A YANKEE CHRISTMAS

&

A YANKEE CHRISTMAS

Featuring Vermont Celebrations

VOLUME 2

feasts, treats, crafts and traditions of wintertime new england

BY SALLY RYDER BRADY

YANKEE BOOKS

Printed in the United States of America.

YANKEE is a registered trademark of Yankee Publishing, Inc. Used by permission.

The quote on page xv, by Howard Thurman, was originally published by the Fellowship of Reconciliation to support its worldwide work for peace and nonviolent action. Reprinted by permission.

"The Bells of Christmas" was previously published in Woman's Day, *December, 1990.*

On the cover: Ice-covered branches on Mount Mansfield in Vermont (background), Christmas Tree Wafers found on page 9 (front inset), dashing through the snow in Burke Mountain, Vermont (back inset).

Library of Congress Cataloging-in-Publication Data

Brady, Sally Ryder
    Featuring Vermont Celebrations : feasts, treats, crafts, and traditions of wintertime New England / by Sally Ryder Brady.
        p.   cm. — (A Yankee Christmas ; v. 2)
    Includes index.
    ISBN 0–89909–366–3 hardcover
    1. Christmas decorations—New England.   2. Handicraft—New England.
    3. Christmas cookery.   I. Title.   II. Series.
    TT900.C4B677   1993
    745.594'12—dc20   93–14198
                                                                                    CIP

Distributed in the book trade by St. Martin's Press

2   4   6   8   10   9   7   5   3   1   hardcover

YANKEE CHRISTMAS EDITORIAL AND DESIGN STAFF

Editor: Sarah Dunn
Managing Editor: Edward Claflin
Executive Editor: Debora Tkac
Art Director: Jane Knutila
Associate Art Director/Book Designer: Debra Sfetsios
Layout Designer: Meg Storm
Production Editor: Jane Sherman
Copy Editor: Ellen Pahl
Photo Editor: Stan Green
Projects and Food Photographer: Angelo Caggiano
Illustrator: Susan Rosenberger
Pattern Illustrator: Nancy Lorenz
Story Illustrator: Doron Ben-Ami
Front Cover Photographers: David Muench (*background*), Angelo Caggiano (*inset*)
Back Cover Photographers: David Muench (*background*), David Brownell (*inset*)
Food Stylist: Mariann Sauvion
Food Prop Stylist: Randi Barritt
Prop Stylist: Marianne Laubach
Gift Basket Stylist: Barbara Fritz

For my parents,
weavers of Christmas magic
from my very first stocking

❧ CONTENTS ❧

ACKNOWLEDGMENTS

I would like thank the following talented and patient contributors to this book: Susan Bates, Elizabeth Berg, Amy Harrison Casey, Madeleine DiCicco, Clint Flagg, Jan Flagg, Cindy Foster, Beth Hylan, Faith Kolodziejski, Kate Kruschwitz, Nina Kruschwitz, New England Nurseries, Kathy Oliver, Jennifer Plant, Mary Skillings, Elizabeth Timmins, Lisa Wallace, Nancy Walton, Bobbie Ward, Neal Ward and Joan Wickersham.

Special thanks as well go to all the generous Vermonters who made this book possible: Kitty Bacon at Six Willows Farm; Lillian Marcotte on Hartland Hill; Max Commins of the Kedron Valley Inn and his chef, Tom Hopewell; Eileen McGuckin at Simon Pearce and chefs Paul Langhans and James Henahan; Debbie Doyle Schectman of Quechee; Bruce McIlveen and Jack Foster at Jackson House; Lou Schmertz at Skunk Hollow Tavern and his chef Carlos Ocasio; Joe del Fino at Old Moses Farm; Tina and Willis Wood; chef Peter J. Wynia, CEC, AAC, at the Woodstock Inn; and Paul Kendall. I am particularly grateful to Mary Louise and Ron Thorburn at the Inn at Weathersfield for their many kindnesses and for welcoming me to their warm hearth.

To Meg Walker at the Shelburne Museum, Kathy Wendling of the Woodstock Historical Society and Susan McKee at Billings Farm and Museum, thank you for opening so many doors into our lively past.

Also, special thanks to all the other elves who helped to make this book special: Bryn, Chris and Damon Sfetsios; the staff at Burnside Plantation; Jake Makosky of Windy Hill Antiques for the loan of his beautiful painting; and the Finnegan family for letting us and our photography equipment into their home.

To Sarah Dunn, tireless miracle worker, a resounding Hallelujah and a sweet Shalom.

PREFACE

a time to believe

When I was a little girl growing up in Woods Hole on Cape Cod, I believed in things that other children scoffed at—fairies, for instance, and angels. I believed in Santa Claus long, long after my friends had stopped. In fact, I remember trying to keep my mother from telling me the truth. A part of me already knew, but still, I didn't want to hear it.

In spite of all logic and rationality and almost 50 years of experience, I am happy to say that I haven't completely grown up. Magic still flickers through my days, and I continue making wishes.

Back in those Santa years, I always wished for snow. One year it happened, a good northeaster just before Christmas. I must have been about nine. My mother let me buy the tree that year, and I set off, pulling my Flexible Flyer behind me, to the village. (In Woods Hole, nothing was very far away.) I can still remember how happy I felt, almost as though I were part of a story. Trudging home through the wet snow, with the too-big tree on my too-small sled, the happiness didn't even begin to fade. If anything, it increased with every soggy step. I felt like a hero; I felt favored.

One of the things that I have always cherished are the dreams of Christmas, especially the dream that for one day, millions of people all over the world would be connected by a shared—if brief—happiness. A part of me still clings to that simple dream. There are other Christmas visions that we probably share—of snowy landscapes and tidy farmhouses, villages clustered around a church with a spire, families gathered around the holiday table.

In New England, most of us have the perfect Christmas stage set even though we can't always count on the snow. The warm old houses, churches, bare maples and graceful evergreens are all here, with winding rivers, a few old covered bridges, rolling fields, winter seashores and cold, starry skies. Now to introduce some of the other elements—the peace, especially, and the active merriment.

One Christmas night a few years ago, my daughter Sarah and I came up with an interesting idea. It had been a long but happy day, with too much food and too many presents, winding up with our usual family and neighborhood buffet late Christmas afternoon. Sarah and I were stretched out in front of the fire.

"Next year, Mom, let's do it differently," she said. "First of all, let's not spend so much money." (Sarah was, at that time, working her way through college.)

"We could all give handmade presents," I said, but my words sounded feeble. That's what Sarah had done, and still her pockets were empty. Then, together, we came to the brilliant idea of only giving each other intangible gifts—a song sung, a dance danced, a story told, a beautiful view pointed out. Nothing that anyone could keep longer than the moment, or the memory of the moment.

I have to confess that we haven't yet been brave enough to carry this out. Alexander, the youngest, was outraged when we told him about it. "It's not fair! All the other guys got good presents when they were my age, like bikes and skis!" Still, every year I hope that this Christmas I have the courage to unhitch a little more from the compulsory gift-giving that advertisers foist on us.

One way to start is to try to make as many gifts as we can, and to make them out of whatever is at hand. New Englanders are legendary savers and scrimpers and inventors. You will find quite a diverse array of easy and thrifty projects here, from refurbishing an old sled (like my Flexible Flyer) to creating a keepsake wreath. Projects such as the sea lavender ball or branch bird feeder can be completed in an hour or two, and others like the clothespin ornaments are perfect for doing with a friend or with a child.

My three holiday trips to Vermont have made me rethink my Christmas. I find myself selecting three or four evergreen boughs— rather than clipping off an armful—for my table. And this year, we only put half the ornaments on the tree, which means they are truly visible. I haven't made as many different kinds of breads and cookies, though I've made the same volume. This way, I have more time to reflect on everyday magic that might pass unnoticed...

I am sitting in my faded red wing chair in the cozy room I use for all my Christmas projects. Around me are leftover bits and pieces of my creations—a few rose hips, a little bunch of dried sea lavender, hanging ribbons, a stray pinecone. The fire is glowing and the house is warm and quiet, though I can hear Upton, my husband, rustling around in the kitchen. It is late afternoon, the light is going fast and the snow has just begun.

I would like to prolong this pre-Christmas moment forever. There is no frenzy here, no shop 'til you drop. Just the happiest hint of Christmas, a buzz of expectation and returning children, a whiff of rising dough. And secrets, swirling in corners. I could sit here all day, watching my thoughts coast by like the lazy snowflakes outside the window. But it's time to bring in some wood, time to close the barn door so the goat won't wander, time to punch down the bread dough.

When I step outside, the world is muffled and I can hear individual snowflakes land. No creature has stepped on the smooth white billow that used to be our lawn and I walk close to the house so my footprints won't show. I feel solitary out here, but not lonely. I feel as though the world were suddenly new, and that this peaceful moment were made only for me.

I get my load of wood, noticing the bark on the logs, and how the inside grain runs in stripes where the logs were split. Time is very slow, I am very slow, the world is white and silent. And for just this moment now, right here, I am safe and at peace. This is a true gift of Christmas, a moment of peace, safety, wholeness. Be on the lookout; be ready to let the moment seize you when it comes.

When the song of the angels is stilled,
When the star in the sky is gone,
When the kings and princes are home,
When the shepherds are back with their flocks,
The work of Christmas begins:
    To find the lost,
    To heal the broken,
    To feed the hungry,
    To release the prisoner,
    To rebuild nations,
    To bring peace among people,
    To make music in the heart.
          —Howard Thurman

Sally Ryder Brady

NEW ENGLAND CHRISTMAS COOKING

tempting soups, breads and treats

As soon as the weather turns cold and my garden is pretty much put to bed (except for a few root vegetables tucked beneath a good hay mulch), I turn to the kitchen. The warmth and smells draw me in, and I feel like an artist in a studio. Food is essential, but when I'm in the thick of holiday baking, the results begin to feel almost like miniature works of art. I like to give homemade presents, and since I am no needleworker and no whiz with paintbrush or stencil, I cook up many of my holiday gifts instead.

Early in December, I get out all my favorite recipes. New and old, they drift across the kitchen table, the counter and the floor. I scan each splattered index card, each scrap of scribbled-on paper, stopping to let the memories of other winters—other holidays— sift in.

This chapter has a smattering of traditional winter food to eat and enjoy and to give away as gifts. The recipes in my files come from family, friends, and the New England kitchens I have been lucky enough to visit. Like other parts of the country, the six New England states have rich, kaleidoscopic mixtures of cultures. If I had begun to tap the traditional holiday cooking brought in from other countries, the selection process would have been unthinkable. So these recipes hail primarily from our Puritan forebears and their English roots.

One of the most important ingredients in every holiday kitchen project is *time*. I hope you will set aside enough time for your holiday cooking so that you can enjoy it. Sometimes I like to work alone as I cook and let my thoughts settle; sometimes I like to be festive and have a friend or a child or two share in the cooking as well as gossip and laughter. Go overboard and make too much—even twice as much—so you can be a generous giver and still have some left for your own household.

Before I go back to my recipe boxes, I'd like to wish you a creative December in an aromatic kitchen, a warm respite from the holiday hustle outside.

TRUE NEW ENGLAND CLAM CHOWDER

There are about as many versions of this favorite warmer-upper as there are ways to make a proper clambake. Quahogs (large, tough clams) make the best chowder, but the smaller littlenecks are also tasty. As for flour, it's my view that it ruins the chowder, so you won't find it in the following recipe.

If you like your chowder really thick and you don't give a hoot about calories or fat, then substitute cream for some of the milk. But never, ever, let the chowder boil. This is delicious served with the Rosemary Country Bread on page 6.

¼ pound salt pork, diced
1 medium onion, chopped
2 large potatoes, peeled and diced
3 cups shucked quahogs or littlenecks (including their liquor)
4 cups milk
Salt
Freshly ground black pepper
Sprinkle of chopped fresh parsley (optional)

Fry the salt pork in a 3-quart saucepan over medium-high heat for 4 to 6 minutes, or until lightly browned and crisp. Remove with a slotted spoon to paper towels or a brown paper bag to drain.

Add the onions to the pan and sauté in the pork fat until the onion is soft and translucent. Remove the onions to paper towels or a brown paper bag to drain. Pour off any fat remaining in the pan. Return the onions to the pan with the potatoes and enough water to cover them by 2 to 3 inches. Bring to a simmer and cook until the potatoes are fork-tender, about 10 to 12 minutes.

While the potatoes are cooking, strain the clams over a bowl and reserve the clam liquor. With a sharp paring knife, remove and discard any black necks from the clams. Coarsely chop the clams. Add the clams and their liquor to the saucepan and cook over medium-low heat for 2 to 3 more minutes. Remove from heat.

Scald the milk in another pan and add to the clams and potatoes. At this point, you can add the salt pork again or leave it out if you prefer. Season with salt and pepper. Garnish with parsley and serve.

Makes 6 servings.

Dip in—and eat your fill. True New England Clam Chowder with a crusty loaf of Rosemary Country Bread (page 6).

BUTTERNUT SQUASH SOUP

After a chilly morning sleigh ride, there's nothing more delicious than returning to a fragrant dining room with steaming bowls of squash soup. This soup also goes well with the Rosemary Country Bread on page 6.

To make the roux: Stir together the butter and flour and bake for 10 minutes in a 350° oven. Set aside.

To make the soup: In a large roasting pan, melt the butter and add the onions, leeks, celery, carrots, garlic, thyme and pepper. Cook over medium heat, stirring from time to time, until the vegetables are golden. Add the squash. Stir well and add the wine, vanilla, bay leaves, maple syrup, sugar, cinnamon and nutmeg.

Put the pan in a 350° oven and bake uncovered until the squash is tender, 45 to 50 minutes. Remove the bay leaves. Press the contents of the pan through a coarse sieve or feed it through a food mill into a large pot. Add the chicken stock and bring to a simmer. Cook for a few minutes. Add roux, a spoonful at a time, stirring after each addition. When the soup begins to thicken, you've added enough roux.

Keep warm until ready to serve. Just before serving, add heavy cream to taste. (I add a generous ½ cup.) Rewarm the soup, and serve immediately.

Makes 10 to 12 servings.

Roux

4	tablespoons melted butter
4	tablespoons flour

Soup

1	stick (¼ pound) butter
1	large onion, diced
1	large leek, cleaned and finely diced
1	cup finely diced celery
2	cups finely diced carrots
2	cloves minced garlic
½	teaspoon dried thyme
1	teaspoon ground white pepper
1½	pounds butternut or other winter squash, peeled, seeded and chopped
1	cup white wine
1	teaspoon vanilla
3	bay leaves
½	cup pure maple syrup
¼	cup brown sugar
1	teaspoon cinnamon
¼	teaspoon nutmeg
2	quarts chicken stock
2–4	tablespoons roux
	Heavy cream (about ½ cup)

Autumn meets winter in this hearty squash soup.

Yeast-risen doughnuts and coffee—the perfect sugaring snack.

LILLIAN MARCOTTE'S DOUGHNUTS

Lillian lives on the same Vermont hill that her family has owned and worked since the Revolution. The first time I tasted one of her doughnuts, it was swimming in an amber pool of maple syrup from Lillian's sugar bush down the road.

In every season, and particularly during sugaring, Lillian tries to keep doughnuts on hand for everyone who drops in, and sometimes she makes four dozen a day. They vanish instantly, prey to those who have been working to gather the syrup.

$^1/_2$	cup sugar
1	cup warm milk
$^1/_8$	teaspoon salt
2–3	tablespoons margarine or butter, melted
1	package active dry yeast
1	egg
$^1/_2$	teaspoon nutmeg (optional)
$3^3/_4$	cups flour (approximate)
	Canola oil or vegetable shortening

In a large bowl, mix together the sugar, milk, salt and margarine or butter. Sprinkle in the yeast and stir until it dissolves. Beat in the egg and add the nutmeg, if desired. Gradually add the flour, stirring until the batter is stiff yet springy. Do not knead the dough.

Cover the bowl and let the dough rise until it doubles in bulk—about an hour in a warm kitchen. If you can wait until the next day, however, put the dough into the refrigerator overnight to rise. It's a lot easier to roll out when it has been allowed to cool this way.

Turn out half the dough on a floured board and roll with a floured rolling pin to a thickness of about $^1/_2$ inch. Cut with a floured doughnut cutter, separate the pieces and place them on a cookie sheet lined with wax paper. Fill a second sheet, using the other half of the dough mixture. Leave the cookie sheet out at room temperature for about 1 hour until the dough doubles again.

Place canola oil or vegetable shortening in a skillet. The oil should be 2 inches deep. Heat to a temperature of 370°. (Test with a thermometer.) Using tongs, place the doughnuts with the risen side down in the oil, leaving plenty of room between the doughnuts.

Fry until brown on one side (watch carefully, as they cook fast), then turn over to brown the other side. The secret to light doughnuts is not to overcrowd the pan. If you leave plenty of room, your doughnuts will be light as a cloud. Drain the doughnuts on absorbent paper (I use brown paper bags). Serve warm—plain, sugared or, best of all, like Lillian's, in a puddle of warm pure maple syrup.

Makes 1½ dozen.

ROSEMARY COUNTRY BREAD

This is my favorite bread to eat with any winter soup. Fresh from the oven, it's moist and delicious, redolent of rosemary on the inside, with a thin, slightly glistening crust. I usually use fresh rosemary, but dried will work just as well. And while the addition of olive oil may not be traditionally New England, I think it perfectly rounds out the rosemary and wheat partnership.

In a large saucepan, heat the milk and water together until quite warm (105°). Remove from heat, add the salt and sugar, and stir. Sprinkle on the yeast and gently stir it in. Let the mixture stand about 5 minutes to allow the yeast to dissolve.

Add ½ cup of the cornmeal, 3 tablespoons of the olive oil, the onion, rosemary, whole wheat flour and about 2 cups of the unbleached flour. Mix together and beat well. Turn out onto a lightly floured board or countertop and knead in enough remaining flour to make the dough just stiff enough to handle easily. Knead for about 3 minutes.

Let the dough rest for 10 minutes beneath an inverted bowl that is lightly oiled with olive oil. Knead again for 10 minutes or until dough is springy and smooth, adding small amounts of flour as needed to keep the dough from sticking.

Return the dough to the oiled bowl, turning the dough to completely coat it with oil. Cover the bowl with a damp dish towel and let the dough rise until doubled in bulk, about 1½ to 2 hours. Punch down and divide it in half, shaping each half into a round loaf. Sprinkle the remaining ¼ cup of cornmeal on a cookie sheet and put the loaves, seam side down, on top. Cover them with the damp towel again, and let them rise for about 45 minutes, or until doubled in bulk.

1	cup milk
1	cup water
2	teaspoons salt
2	tablespoons sugar
1	package active dry yeast
¾	cup cornmeal
4	tablespoons virgin olive oil
⅔	cup finely diced onions
2	tablespoons minced fresh rosemary or 2 teaspoons dried
1½	cups whole wheat flour
3–3½	cups unbleached flour
½	cup wheat germ
1	teaspoon kosher salt

Moonrise over a snow-capped barn in Thetford, Vermont.

With a sharp knife, gash an "X" on the top of each loaf. Brush the tops with olive oil and sprinkle on some of the wheat germ and salt. Bake the loaves at 350° until they have turned a nice brown and sound hollow when you rap on them, approximately 30 to 40 minutes. Lightly brush the tops again with olive oil and cool slightly on a wire rack. Eat this bread while it's still warm—there's nothing better!

Makes 2 loaves.

UPTON'S ALMOND SHORTBREAD COOKIES

Every Christmas, my husband, Upton, makes several batches of these cookies to give away. The advantage of short-bread dough is that it can always be prepared ahead and kept in the refrigerator or freezer. Ten minutes after guests arrive, you can have a plateful of warm cookies ready to serve.

In a large mixing bowl, cream the butter and sugar together until they are well blended. Stir in the ground almonds. Sift together the flour, baking powder and salt and gradually add to the butter mixture, stirring well to blend thoroughly.

If you want to bake the cookies now, shape the dough into balls about an inch in diameter and place on a greased cookie sheet. Flatten with a fork dipped in hot water. Place a whole unblanched almond in the center of each cookie. Bake at 350° for about 10 minutes, or until the cookies are an even medium brown.

If you want to store the dough to bake at a later time, form it into logs about 2 inches in diameter and wrap them tightly in plastic wrap. The dough will keep in the refrigerator for up to 2 weeks, or in the freezer for 6 months. If dough is frozen, slice the cookies directly off the log instead of forming them into balls.

Variation: To give a more festive look for Christmas, arrange five almonds in the center of each cookie in a star shape.

Makes about 5 dozen 2-inch cookies.

1	cup butter
⅔	cup light brown sugar
2	cups ground almonds (finely ground for delicate cookies; coarsely ground for crunchy cookies)
2	cups flour
½	teaspoon baking powder
½	teaspoon salt
60	or more whole unblanched almonds

HARDLY DRY FRUIT

You can "plump" currants, raisins, dried cherries and dried cranberries in various kinds of liquor, to the benefit of the dried fruit and the liquor. I pour the fruit into clean glass jars with tight lids and cover them with liquor. Brandy works well with currants and raisins, dark rum seems to enhance cranberries and bourbon is fine with cherries. Or go ahead and experiment with your own combinations.

CINNAMON STARS

My sister claims she can never successfully use a rolling pin. This is the perfect cookie for her and others like her, since this is a dough to be hand-patted, not rolled. The recipe is simple, and the cookies are both pretty and delicious. The only hazard is humidity—don't try to make or store these stars in a moist kitchen.

In a large bowl, whip or whisk the egg whites just until they hold a stiff peak. (Don't let them become dry.) Add the salt, and then the sugar, 1 tablespoon at a time, whipping constantly. Whip in the cinnamon and the lemon zest.

Set aside one-third of this mixture. Gently fold the ground nuts into the other two-thirds of the mixture. Dust a pastry board, pastry cloth or the countertop with confectioners' sugar. With a rubber spatula, turn out the egg/nut mixture. Lightly dust your hands with confectioners' sugar and pat the dough until it is a little less than ½ inch thick. Cut into stars (or other shapes, if you wish). Paint the tops with the reserved egg mixture. Place the stars on a buttered cookie sheet and bake at 300° for 15 to 20 minutes, or until lightly browned.

Makes about 50 1½-inch stars.

5   large egg whites
    Pinch of salt
2   cups confectioners'
    sugar, sifted
2½ teaspoons cinnamon
1½ teaspoons finely
    grated lemon zest
1   pound finely ground
    unblanched almonds
    or hazelnuts

Sweet temptations—Cinnamon Stars, Christmas Tree Wafers and Upton's Almond Shortbread Cookies (page 7).

CHRISTMAS TREE WAFERS

The Christmas I had four children all under the age of five, I was also blessed with a plethora of teenagers who lived across the field and across the street. Whenever any of them wanted to get from one house to the other, they would, to my delight, traipse through my kitchen. These were extraordinary teenagers from large families—kids who loved babies and baking and who would never pass through without lending a hand. One of them showed us how to make these trees. In this recipe I use cream cheese to make a dough that rolls out wafer thin.

½	cup unsalted butter
1	cup sugar
1	large egg, beaten
3	ounces softened cream cheese
2	tablespoons plain yogurt
1½	teaspoons vanilla
2	cups flour
¼	teaspoon baking soda
½	teaspoon baking powder
½	teaspoon salt
1	teaspoon sugar
¼	teaspoon cinnamon
	Seedless red jam
	Confectioners' sugar for sprinkling (optional)

In a large bowl, cream the butter and sugar together. Mix in the egg until blended. Blend the cream cheese, yogurt and vanilla into the butter mixture. Add the flour, baking soda, baking powder and salt, mixing well.

Form the dough into one or more 2-inch logs, wrap well and chill for at least 4 hours in the refrigerator. Roll out very thin on a well-floured board with a well-floured rolling pin. Cut into tree shapes. Combine the sugar and cinnamon and sprinkle on top of the cutouts.

Bake about 9 minutes in a 350° oven. Remove the trees from the oven and, working very quickly with a plastic straw, make holes here and there on half of the trees. Return the trees to the oven until baked, about another 3 minutes. Let the trees cool slightly, then spread the trees *without* the holes with seedless red jam (raspberry or strawberry works well). Dust the trees *with* holes with powdered sugar, if desired, and place on top of the jam trees, like little sandwiches. The jam will squeeze up through the holes and the trees will look as though they have been decorated.

Makes about 3 dozen cookies.

Horse-drawn sleighs cross a meadow at twilight in Woodstock, Vermont.

NEWPORT CHRISTMAS PLUM PUDDING

Plum puddings make excellent presents, especially if you pack them in handsome old bowls. While there are many variations, I like this one best because of its history. The recipe came to Newport, Rhode Island, from England in about 1730, and it has been stirred up by Trinity Church parishioners ever since. You can buy one at the church's annual Christmas bazaar. This recipe produces a bonanza of puddings—five or six if you use modest-sized bowls—so you'll have a few to give away. The flavor improves with age and reheating. I usually enclose the reheating instructions on the back of my gift tag.

To make the pudding: Mix the dry ingredients together in a large mixing bowl. Add the suet and fruits and mix well. In a separate bowl, beat the eggs thoroughly and add the lemon rind and juice, brandy and cider. Add to the previous ingredients and mix well.

Grease 3 large ovenproof pudding bowls or 5 or 6 smaller ones. (If you don't have pudding bowls, use soufflé dishes or even clean coffee cans.) Place the pudding batter into bowls, making sure the bowls are no more than two-thirds full. Cover the bowls with parchment, buttered muslin, double-heavy wax paper or aluminum foil and tie the cover tightly around the top of the bowl with string.

Place the bowls on a rack in a large pot or double boiler and steam for 3 hours. Remove from the pot and let cool. They are now ready to be stored or given away; they should be reheated before they are eaten. Keep the pudding tightly covered, and store at room temperature. (Reminder: When you give away a pudding, be sure to provide serving instructions.)

To serve the pudding: Reheat the pudding by steaming it, covered, for about an hour. Turn it out of its bowl onto a plate (we use a round silver tray) and, if you like, stick a sprig of holly in the top. Heat ¼ to ½ cup of brandy in a flameproof container, ignite it and pour it, flaming, over the pudding.

For a real spectacle, we turn out the dining room lights and make a grand entry with the ignited pudding. But be very careful—when the holly sprig ignites you will have quite a blaze. Serve the pudding with brandy and hard sauces.

To make the brandy sauce: In a small saucepan, cream together the butter and sugar. Add the eggs and cream and cook until slightly thickened, but do not boil. Add the vanilla and brandy. You can make this early in the day and reheat over hot water at the last minute.

To make the hard sauce: In a small bowl, cream together the butter and 2 cups of sugar until very light and fluffy. Blend in the vanilla and bourbon to taste (if you add the full amount of bourbon, you will probably need the additional ½ cup of sugar). Add salt if you like. Chill until ready to serve. You can make this at least a day ahead.

Makes 5 or 6 puddings and 1½ cups of each sauce.

Pudding

- 1   pound (about 4 cups) fine, dry bread crumbs
- 1   pound (4 cups) flour
- 1   pound (2 cups) sugar
- 1   teaspoon salt
- 1   tablespoon cinnamon
- 2   whole nutmegs, grated
- 2   pounds finely chopped or ground suet
- 2   pounds currants
- 2   pounds seedless raisins (I use all or half golden raisins.)
- ½   pound mixed, chopped candied peel
- 2   cups peeled, chopped, apples
- 12 eggs
-     Grated rind and juice of 2 lemons
- ½   cup brandy
- 1   cup sweet cider

Brandy Sauce

- ⅓   cup butter, softened
- 1   cup sugar
- 2   eggs, beaten
- 1   cup heavy cream
- 1   teaspoon vanilla
- 4   tablespoons brandy

Hard Sauce

- ½   cup unsalted butter, softened
- 2–2½ cups sifted confectioners' sugar
- 1   teaspoon vanilla
- 1–4 tablespoons bourbon whiskey
- ⅛   teaspoon of salt (optional)

THE STIRRING OF THE PUDDING

The stirring of the plum pudding is an old tradition that takes place on the Sunday before Advent begins, called "the Last Sunday in Ordinary Time." After church, worshipers file into the parish house and each in turn stirs up the large vat of Christmas pudding batter that stands near the entrance while reciting the Collect at right.

Each person makes a wish while taking a turn. When the pudding is completely stirred, it is then spooned into bowls and sold to the parishioners, and the money collected is used to feed the hungry.

Stir up, we beseech thee, O Lord, the hearts of thy faithful people; that they, plenteously bringing forth the fruit of good works, may by thee be plenteously rewarded; Amen.

—From the Book of Common Prayer

Plum pudding—perfect as a gift or as a flaming centerpiece (see page xvi).

GINGERBREAD SLEIGH

Once upon a time, Cindy Foster was my children's favorite babysitter. Now a mother of two, Cindy is a well-known designer and baker of gingerbread houses. She designed this graceful sleigh in her Maine kitchen and promises that it is easy to make. For a perfect holiday centerpiece, fill the sleigh with petits fours, ginger cookies or Christmas candy. Do not store this in a humid room or the gingerbread will become soft and start to sag. The patterns for the sleigh are on page 14. You will need heavy cardboard for the patterns.

To prepare the gingerbread dough: Sift together the flour, cinnamon, ginger and salt in a large bowl. In a medium saucepan, stir together the corn syrup, brown sugar and margarine until well mixed. Cook over medium heat, stirring constantly, until the margarine is melted. Stir this mixture into the flour mixture until well blended. Let the dough cool until it is easy to handle.

To prepare the pieces: Enlarge and trace the patterns on page 14 and transfer them to heavy cardboard. (See "How to Enlarge a

Gingerbread Dough

6½	cups flour
1½	tablespoons cinnamon
1½	teaspoons ginger
1	teaspoon salt
1½	cups light or dark corn syrup
1¼	cups light brown sugar
1	cup margarine or butter

Candies out for a ride in a Gingerbread Sleigh.

Pattern" on page 14.) Cut them out and set them aside.

Line a cookie sheet with foil. Place one-third of the dough on the lined cookie sheet and roll it into a rectangular shape, approximately ¼ inch thick.

Arrange the cardboard sleigh patterns on the dough, leaving at least 1 inch between pieces. With a sharp knife, carefully cut around each piece. Remove the cardboard patterns, pull up the excess dough and repeat the entire process to make all the needed pieces.

To bake the pieces: Bake the individual sleigh pieces (still on the foil) at 350° for 20 to 25 minutes, or until the gingerbread is lightly browned. (It should feel firm when you touch it lightly with your finger.) Remove the cookie sheet from the oven and place it on a wire rack to cool. After the gingerbread has completely cooled, remove it from the foil.

To prepare the icing: Using a mixer set at low speed, beat all the ingredients in a large mixing bowl until smooth. Then beat at high speed for 7 to 10 minutes or until the icing is stiff (when a knife drawn through leaves a path). For stiffer icing, beat in more confectioners' sugar. The icing dries very quickly, so be sure to keep the bowl tightly covered with plastic wrap. If necessary, you can store the icing overnight at room temperature in an airtight container—beat it again before using.

To assemble the sleigh: Fill a pastry bag with icing. The general procedure for joining the pieces is to pipe the icing onto the adjoining surfaces, prop the pieces in place and let them dry. If you don't have a pastry tube, use a small spatula or dull knife to spread on the icing.

On a cookie sheet, assemble the base of the sleigh by attaching the 2 braces crosswise between the 2 runners (keep the smooth sides—the top of the gingerbread—facing out). Support the runners with jars or cans during assembly. Allow to dry (about 30 to 60 minutes, depending on the humidity).

Assemble the body of the sleigh without the icing to check the fit. Trim the pieces as necessary for a good, tight fit, scraping off any rough edges or protrusions with a dull knife. Then, when the pieces fit, you can assemble the sleigh with icing.

Raise the bottom of the sleigh above the cookie sheet by resting it on several bottle caps. Ice the edges of the bottom, then place the sides in position, propping them in place with heavy jars or cans. Ice the edges of the front and back, and place them in the sleigh at an angle. Allow to dry.

Ice the top edges of the base assembly. Place the body of the sleigh on top. Allow to dry.

To decorate the sleigh: Using a pastry bag, decorate the sleigh with the remaining icing. (If you want colored decorations, mix food coloring into small batches of the icing. Thin the icing with drops of water if necessary.) Fill the sleigh with cookies, candies or decorations for a charming holiday centerpiece.

Makes 1 sleigh.

Ornamental Icing

- 1 pound (3¼ cups) confectioners' sugar
- 3 egg whites (at room temperature)
- ½ teaspoon cream of tartar

  Food coloring (optional)

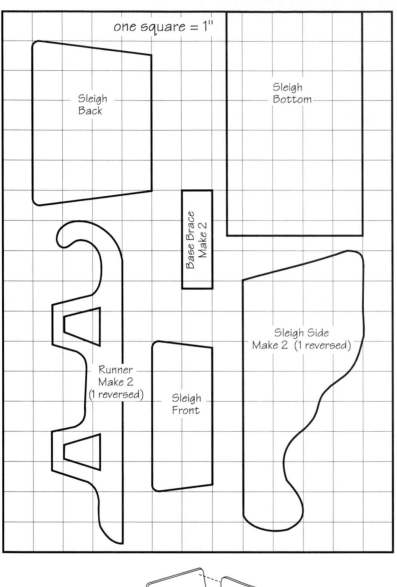

one square = 1"

Sleigh Back

Sleigh Bottom

Base Brace Make 2

Runner Make 2 (1 reversed)

Sleigh Front

Sleigh Side Make 2 (1 reversed)

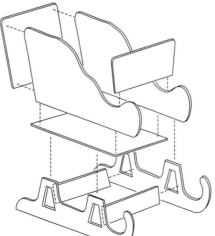

Patterns and assembly for Gingerbread Sleigh.

HOW TO ENLARGE A PATTERN

The patterns in this book have been reduced in size and keyed to a grid. You can easily enlarge the patterns by using a photocopier or referring to the grid.

Using a photocopier: *A photocopy service will enlarge the pattern. To double the size of the pattern, ask for a 200% enlargement. The enlarged pattern can be printed on paper or transparent vellum.*

Using the grid as reference: *First, draw a new grid on a sheet of paper. (It's easiest to use graph paper.) Make each square of the grid the size indicated. If 1 square = 1 inch, draw the grid lines 1 inch apart.*

Mark the new grid with reference letters and numbers. Indicate with pencil dots where the lines of the pattern cross the lines of the grid. Using the dots as reference, carefully redraw the full-size pattern.

Transferring the pattern: *The easiest way to transfer the pattern is to cut it out of heavy paper, posterboard or oak tag. If you will be using it many times, it's helpful to make several patterns ahead of time so that as they wear out or become too stained to use, you already have replacements. Trace around your patterns, taking care, if necessary, to ensure that your lines are light enough that they won't show when your project is completed.*

Fragrant and sweet treat—a taste of summer on a winter day.

BEN AND JERRY AND SALLY'S LAVENDER HONEY ICE CREAM

Vermont-based Ben and Jerry have done for ice cream what Santa in the North Pole did for stockings. And with this recipe, you can share in the bounty. The basic ice cream recipe is Ben and Jerry's; the lavender honey idea is mine.

You may think it odd to have ice cream in a wintertime book, but once I ate an ice cream cone in a kind of crude igloo a friend and I had made—it was the best ice cream ever, and it lasted and lasted outside in the frosty air. The ice cream here will remind you of summer—fragrant with lavender, sweet with honey—and is a splendid companion to the Almond Angel Cake found on page 74.

1	cup whole milk
1	tablespoon crushed fresh or dried lavender blossoms
3	tablespoons honey
2	large eggs
$\frac{1}{2}$	cup sugar
2	cups heavy cream
$1\frac{1}{2}$	teaspoons vanilla

Heat the milk almost to boiling in a small, heavy-bottomed saucepan. Stir in the lavender and honey and let sit, covered, until completely cool. Chill one hour or more in refrigerator.

Whisk the eggs in a bowl until light and fluffy, 1 to 2 minutes. Whisk in the sugar a little at a time, then continue whisking until completely blended, about a minute or more. Strain the lavender milk and whisk into the eggs and sugar. Whisk in the cream and vanilla.

Freeze your ice cream according to the directions accompanying your ice cream maker.

Makes 1 quart.

CHAPTER TWO

NEWFOUND GIFTS
FROM
HAND-ME-DOWNS

crafts and keepsakes from bygone years

⚬

The more I travel and talk to people—from the northern borders of Maine to the southern shores of Rhode Island and Connecticut—the more I see a shift away from the new and back to the old, from buying to making.

Like children, we are so often drawn to what is new and shiny that it is easy to forget the more simple and less eye-catching aspects of Christmas. In my travels through New England, I have met a host of people who continue to quietly pass along to the next generation traditions and skills they learned from their parents or grandparents. These are the people who keep our pasts present—and we owe them a lot. The only way I know of reciprocating is to give someone else one of the easy hand-me-downs you'll find here. Here's *your* chance to make, rather than buy, some of the gifts you pass along this Christmas.

CLOTHESPIN ORNAMENTS

I can remember my mother making clothespin people for me when I was small, and I did the same for my own children. This year, I was only going to make a ballerina, an angel and a soldier, but when I invited my friend Kate Kruschwitz to help, she showed me how to transform some tired old artificial flowers into delicious little "petal people."

Ballerina

1. Paint the face (skin, cheeks, mouth, eyes), legs and shoes on the clothespin. Let dry. Cut short (2-inch) lengths of pipe cleaner for arms and glue them on.

2. For modesty's sake, cut a piece of fabric or wide ribbon and glue it on as an underskirt. (If you want to get really fancy, hem the lower edge.) Then glue on the frilly skirt, in layers if you like. Choose fancy ribbon or beading for the top of the ballerina costume and glue it on. Allow the glue to dry.

3. Glue on lambs' wool for the hair—a small clump for short hair; a larger clump for long, flowing hair. Or, as an alternative, use embroidery thread (one ballerina shown in the photograph has blond hair made from yellow thread that was arranged and then glued on).

4. Finish your ballerina by gluing on ribbons for her slipper laces. Then adorn her as you like with glued-on tiny flowers, beads, ribbons and other trimmings to dress her up for your special ballet.

Materials for Ballerina

Clothespin (I prefer the kind with pointed ends for feet)

White, beige, pink, blue and brown craft paint

Small paintbrush

Glue gun

Pipe cleaner

Assorted scraps of fabric, including gauze, netting or lace

Assorted sequins, tiny flowers, pearls, ribbons and other trimmings

Lambs' wool (available in most drugstores)

Narrow ribbon or gold thread

The world of a windowsill can be home to your family of clothespin people.

5. Tie a 6-inch piece of narrow ribbon into a loop and glue or tie it to the ballerina so she can dance from the limbs of your tree.

Angel

1. Paint the face (skin, cheeks, mouth, eyes) and legs on the clothespin. Let dry. Cut short (2-inch) lengths of pipe cleaner for arms and glue them on.

2. Glue on the angel's dress—in as many layers as you like. Add flowing overskirts and ribbons if you want her to be fancy. Then glue on lace or feather wings. (To make an angel wing, gather up a loop of gauzy fabric into a small bow, then glue it on, allowing one end of the fabric to fall below the wing. Repeat for the other wing.) Allow the glue to dry.

3. Glue on lambs' wool for the hair—a small clump for short hair; a larger clump for long, flowing hair. Or, as an alternative, use embroidery thread (one angel shown has beautiful golden hair made from thread that was glued onto the top of her head). Add a halo by gluing it only on the back of the angel's head and letting it float in a heavenly manner above her hair.

4. Tie a 6-inch piece of gold thread into a loop and glue or tie it to the angel. Hang her on your tree, from the mantel or in a window.

Soldier

1. Paint the face (skin, cheeks, mouth, eyes and hat strap). Let the paint dry completely. (When painting the soldier, make sure each color is completely dry before going on to the next.) Paint his legs blue or black. Add his red jacket, then his hands and cross-straps.

2. Glue on the pom-pom hat, using quite a bit of glue to secure all the fibers around his face. Let dry completely.

3. Using a 6-inch length of ribbon, tie your soldier onto a handy branch of your tree (preferably near a ballerina so they can dance the night away).

Petal Person

1. Paint the face (skin, cheeks, mouth, eyes) and legs on the clothespin. Let dry. Cut short (2-inch) lengths of pipe cleaner for arms and glue them on.

2. Disassemble the flower, then select petals and glue them to the clothespin. Attach the petals upside down for her skirt, then the leaves (also upside down) for her bodice. Trim large leaves or petals or use small ones for her bonnet.

3. Add assorted trimmings to make her fancy or more sophisticated— we gave our petal people lace collars, "bouquets" of lavender mixed with stamens left over from the flowers, and tiny blossoms to accent the bonnets.

4. Tie a 6-inch piece of gold thread into a loop and glue or tie it to the petal person. If you want, spray her with a little perfume to add to her floral mystique.

Materials for Angel

Clothespin

White, beige, pink, blue and brown craft paint

Small paintbrush

Glue gun

Pipe cleaner

Assorted scraps of white fabric, gauze, netting and lace

Feathers

Gold cord, ribbon or pearls for halo

Lambs' wool (available in most drugstores)

Gold thread

Materials for Soldier

Clothespin

White, beige, pink, blue, red and black craft paint

Small paintbrush

Glue gun

Black pom-pom

Narrow ribbon

Materials for Petal Person

Clothespin

White, beige, pink, blue and brown craft paint

Small paintbrush

Glue gun

Pipe cleaner

Artificial flower

Assorted sequins, tiny flowers, pearls, ribbons and other trimmings

Gold thread

Covered beads—a beautiful garland for your tree.

COVERED BEAD GARLAND

I first saw covered beads in Hyannis, Massachusetts, made by a woman who said that her elderly mother in Connecticut had made beads such as these ever since she was a child. Since then I have seen similar beads throughout New England. You can make covered beads into a striking garland for your tree—this one is 6 feet long. Note that the larger beads will be covered by fabric, so they can be wood or plastic in any color or a multitude of colors. But the smaller beads will show—so keep that in mind when you're selecting them, and make sure they have a hole large enough for the fabric to go through.

1. Fold the fabric lengthwise with wrong sides together and sew a very narrow seam along the long side to make a tube. (Because the fabric gathers, it won't matter that you don't sew it inside out—just make sure there are no loose threads hanging.) Make sure that the inside of the tube is slightly larger than the ½-inch beads.

2. String on a small bead about 1½ inches from one end of the tube. Then slide a large bead into the tube, up against the small bead. Continue alternating small beads on the outside of the tube with large beads on the inside, ending with a small bead 1½ inches from the other end.

3. Finish the ends of the tube by tying knots in the ends of the fabric, and hang the garland on your tree.

Materials

85 large beads, ½" diameter

86 small beads, ⅜" diameter

1½" × 7' strip of lightweight fabric

GREAT GRANDDADDY'S BRANCH BIRD FEEDER

When Clint Flagg was growing up on the family farm in Connecticut, he was surrounded by an extended family, all of them busy. But none was too busy to take a minute to show a child the beauty of a lichen-covered log or uses for a dead branch. Years later, Clint remembered to add branch bird feeders in the "hidden garden" outside his studio shop in Hyannis, Massachusetts. For what is a garden without birds?

1. Nail or screw the two 9-inch branches to one of the 12-inch branches to form the tray, as shown. Attach the 30-inch branches to each other at the top, then nail or screw the remaining 12-inch branch across the bottom to form the frame. Attach the tray to the frame. Attach the screening to the underside of the tray with nails, staples or thin wire as needed. Nail or screw the 24-inch branches inside the frame, as shown.

2. Fill the screen with bird seed or sunflower seed mix.

3. Hang the feeder on a fence or the side of your barn, but make sure you put it where you can watch the birds enjoy your hospitality.

Simple and rustic—every Branch Bird Feeder is unique.

Materials

2 9" green maple branches for tray sides, twigs and leaves removed

2 12" green maple branches for tray front and back, twigs and leaves removed

2 30" green maple branches, twigs and leaves removed

2 24" green maple branches for inside frame, leaves only removed

8–12 small nails or screws

Staple gun and staples

12" × 18" piece of nylon screening

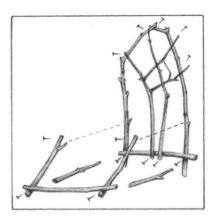

Nail the branches together to form the tray and frame.

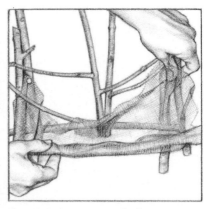

Attach the screening to the frame.

Spice-Filled Mug Mats release a soothing fragrance.

SPICE-FILLED MUG MATS

Our New England ancestors kept their houses tightly closed against the winter chill, but they also knew how to keep those houses smelling fresh all winter long with fragrant herbs and spices. These mug mats serve a delightful double surprise. They're coasters that protect the tabletop from heat and moisture, and as soon as they're touched by the warmth of a steaming mug, they release their fragrance. Jan Flagg, who works with her husband, Clint, designing secret gardens and fairy houses, makes these in her herb-filled Cape Cod studio (often helped by her two young daughters). The materials listed are enough for six mug mats. For a wintery gift, fill a small basket with a mug mat or two, cider spices or tea bags, a pretty mug and a few cookies.

1. Cut a 6¼-inch square from each of the printed fabric, muslin and batting. Place the printed fabric on a flat surface, right side up. Place the muslin square on top of the fabric square. Place the cotton batting on top of the muslin square.

2. Sew the pieces together with a ⅝-inch seam allowance and leave a 2-inch opening on one side. Trim the corners and turn the mat right side out through the opening so that the print is on one side and the muslin is on the other. Press lightly. Topstitch ¼ inch in from the edge around the three closed sides.

3. Mix all the spices and the oils together in a small bowl. Through the 2-inch opening, fill the mat with a tablespoon of the spice mixture. Place it between the batting and the print fabric. Blindstitch the seam opening and topstitch ¼ inch in from the edge across the fourth side.

Materials

¼ **yard printed fabric**

¼ **yard undyed sailcloth or heavy muslin**

¼ **yard ¼" cotton batting**

2 tablespoons whole cloves

2 tablespoons coriander seed

1 tablespoon crushed cinnamon sticks

1 tablespoon sandalwood chips (optional)

1 tablespoon whole allspice

A few drops oil of cinnamon

A few drops oil of vanilla

Leave 2" opening

Batting

Muslin

Fabric

Sew the three layers together.

PEQUOT LAVENDER WAND

Almost anyone who has lavender growing in the garden will want to make some of these wands to tuck in a drawer or hide inside a stocking. Their fragrance becomes part of Christmas magic. I learned this uncomplicated procedure for making Pequot lavender wands from Clint Flagg, who learned it from his Connecticut grandmother. To bring out the lavender scent, Clint suggests holding the wand in your hand to warm it. Then wave it through your room, and you will walk in fragrance for hours to come.

1. Hold the lavender in your left hand, with all the blossoms at the same height. Twist the wire or thread tightly around all the stalks just below the end of the blossoms.

2. Turn the lavender upside down, so the flower tops point down, and gently fold the stems, one by one, over the wire and down, radiating all around the blossoms as if you were encasing them in a cage made of the stems.

3. When all the stems are folded down, twist another piece of wire or thread around them all just below the top of the blossoms. Wind a ribbon around the stalks and tie in a bow.

Simple sprigs of lavender make pretty scented wands.

Materials

10 long stalks of fresh lavender flowers

Very thin florist's wire or gold thread

Narrow ribbon

Tie the stems together just below the blossoms.

Fold the stems down around the blossoms and tie the stems again.

DOVE ORNAMENT

Lisa Colt, a gifted teacher, artist and writer from Dedham, Massachusetts, used to make these dove ornaments for her four young boys during the dark days of the Vietnam War. She passed the pattern to me, along with her continuing hopes for a peaceful world.

Materials

Old Christmas card
Glue
Thread

1. The patterns can be enlarged or reduced to make different-size doves (see "How to Enlarge a Pattern" on page 14). Trace the patterns onto the card and cut out the pieces. You will need one body piece, two wings and two tabs. Fold the tabs in half.

2. Glue half of a tab to each side of the body where indicated by the dotted line. When the glue dries, glue the wings in place on the other half of the tabs.

3. Glue thread onto the body at the X and let your dove fly among the branches of your Christmas tree.

Dove Ornament patterns and assembly.

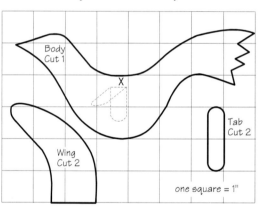
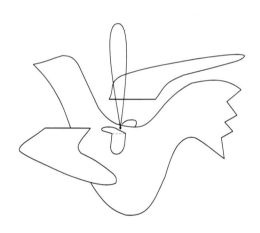

A perfect project for children—graceful doves made from Christmas cards.

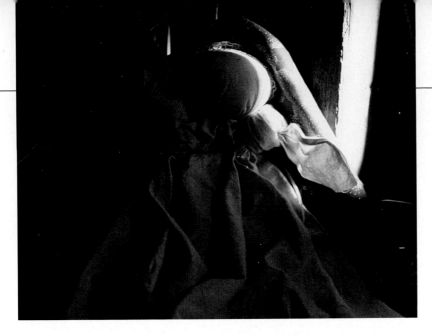

No child (or adult) can resist this sweet Baby Doll.

BABY DOLL

Generations of New England grandmothers and great-grandmothers have soothed fussy babies with these simple dolls, which you can make in less time than it takes to sing "Away in a Manger." For the fabric, you can use a dishtowel, diaper or any large piece of nonbulky material, adding a scrap of lace and a few stitches to "fancy up" the baby a bit. Make the doll as small or as large as you wish, and don't worry if the muslin or other fabric isn't quite square. The baby pictured above was made from a 24-inch square of unbleached muslin.

1. Lay the fabric flat and fold one side over about 6 inches. Wad up an old stocking or other filler into a fist-size ball and place under the fold, about halfway across the side. This is the baby's head.

2. Gather the folded material on one side of the head and tie a knot in the fabric to make one arm. Repeat on the other side of the head to make the other arm. Turn the baby over so the fold is in back.

3. Tie the ribbon in a bow around the baby's neck. If you want to dress up your baby, tack on lace to frame the face like a bonnet.

Materials

24" square of muslin or other fabric

An old nylon stocking or other filler for head

12" narrow satin ribbon

6" piece of lace

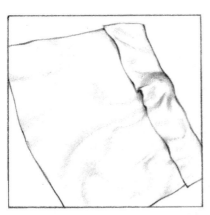

Place the stuffing material under the fold.

Tie a knot for the baby's arm; repeat for the other arm.

Sew lace to the baby's head to make a dressy bonnet.

CHAPTER THREE

WASTE NOT, WANT NOT

handicrafts from attic treasures

*L*ike many New England children, I grew up with the "waste not, want not" refrain echoing in my ears. My thrifty mother still saves bits of string, darns socks and table linens, and even washes paper plates to use again. No wonder that when I became a mother, I used to sew a parade of buttons down my children's overall straps so that sprouting toddlers could wear them longer (knees patched, of course).

Even now, we resist throwing away anything that might be useful or reusable. On Christmas and birthdays, we carefully smooth and refold each piece of used wrapping paper, removing the

A wintertime skating party on Bradley Lake in Andover, New Hampshire.

tape with utmost care. Meticulously, we rewind wrinkled ribbons to be used again.

In the same way, worn-out clothes too raggedy to be worn by another child can turn into pillows or patchwork before they become rags, and other people's cast-off tables and toys can be reborn with a little sanding and a coat of paint. When our four children were young and our wallets were slim, I would spend many a November and December morning, while the children were safely in school, searching for outgrown skis, boots, skates (and one year outgrown ponies!) for December 25th. These secondhand objects (ponies not included) would get spruced up in the cellar, while the children, knowing something was afoot, hovered at top of the cellar stairs. I remember putting endless coats of black shoe paint on a pair of white figure skates for Andrew. On Christmas morning, they glowed like ebony under the tree, but after a few hours on Andrew's flailing feet, the insistent white broke right back through, to Andrew's and my dismay.

Even though I've given up disguising skates for good, I wholeheartedly recommend the refurbishing and reclamation projects in this chapter. Though many of them start with secondhand goods, you will end up with heirlooms once you've worked your magic on flea-market finds.

CHECKERBOARD TABLE

A Houdini of the flea-market crowd, Nancy Walton of Burlington, Massachusetts, can do magic with old objects found in attics and at garage sales. For proof, just look what she did to transform the shabby table that came from her grandmother's attic. The cheerful checkerboard top with its apple counters is bound to please players and nonplayers alike.

1. Prepare the table by sanding off all old, flaking paint or varnish. Make sure the surface is smooth and free of any loose material.

2. Clean the table thoroughly by wiping it with a rag dampened with mineral spirits.

3. When the table is completely dry, apply a coat of primer.

4. When the primer has completely dried, apply the final coat of paint.

Materials

Old end table

Sandpaper, medium and fine

Rag

Mineral spirits

Paintbrush

1 pint latex primer

1 pint latex interior paint

2 pieces (8½" × 11" each) of Mylar

X-Acto knife

Red, green and brown acrylic stencil paint

Stencil brushes

Masking tape

16 small unpainted wooden apples (available at craft stores)

Red and pale green craft paint

With paint and stencils, transform a table into a checkerboard.

5. For general stenciling instructions, see "Basic Stenciling Technique" on page 36. Enlarge the checkerboard pattern onto a piece of Mylar, following the instructions in "How to Enlarge a Pattern" on page 14. Our squares are 2¼ inches each, but you can make them larger or smaller to accommodate the size of your table. (You will stencil the pattern four times, making a complete checkerboard.)

6. Cut out the stencil.

7. Measure the table and carefully position the stencil so that your completed checkerboard will be centered on the tabletop.

8. Tape the stencil onto the table and paint the alternating red squares. Wipe the stencil clean. Let the paint dry.

9. Repeat three times to complete the checkerboard pattern.

10. Enlarge the tree pattern as you did the checkerboard and transfer it to the other piece of Mylar. Cut out the stencil.

11. Tape the tree stencil across one end of the table, again making sure the stencil is centered.

12. Paint the stencil.

13. Repeat taping and painting of the tree stencil across the other end of the table.

14. Apply a coat of primer to the apple counters, and let dry. Paint eight apples red and the other eight pale green.

Stencil patterns for the Checkerboard Table.

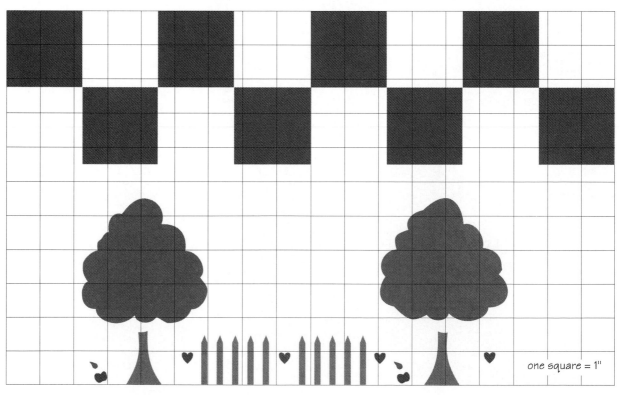

one square = 1"

Any collector of stuffed animals will love this hand-me-down raccoon.

STUFFED RACCOON

You can make Mr. Raccoon out of old corduroy pants or an outgrown velvet dress or even a threadbare tweed. Then look for scraps of contrasting fabric to use for the paws, face and tail. The pattern came from Catherine Oliver in Riverdale, Rhode Island, who often dresses her raccoons in little sweaters and knit hats made from worn-out big sweaters. The actual raccoon pictured here was made by Cindy Foster in Cumberland, Maine, who also made the Gingerbread Sleigh found on page 12.

1. Enlarge the patterns on pages 33 and 34 to full size, following the instructions in "How to Enlarge a Pattern" on page 14.

The pattern pieces are drawn so that the *right* side of the body will be constructed using the pieces as shown. *Each pattern piece will need to be flipped over and cut out separately for the left side of the body.* (Note that you will cut only one head gusset and that you will cut four legs. The leg patterns shown are for the right sides of each leg.)

Materials

½ **yard or scraps of dark brown corduroy (body)**

Scraps of light brown corduroy (face and end of tail)

Scraps of black velvet (paws and middle of tail)

Scraps of fur (ears and eyelashes)

2 black 12mm safety eyes (available at craft stores)

Polyester fiberfill

8 two-hole flat buttons, ³/₄" diameter

Black embroidery thread

Embroidery needle

Pin the pattern pieces to the right side of the fabric, matching the arrows on the pattern pieces to the grain of the fabric. Transfer all markings on the patterns and cut out the pieces. Then flip the pattern pieces, still on the right side of the fabric, and repeat.

2. Throughout, when sewing, use a scant ¼-inch seam, always sewing with the right sides of the fabric together. Clip seams only where indicated, and finger-press the seams open as you go.

3. *To make the head:* Sew the right mask to the right cheek. Then add the right nose section. Add the right side front, as shown at right. Repeat with the pieces for the left side. Sew the completed halves together, stitching from point A to point B. Add the head gusset, sewing from point A to point C on both sides of the head.

Turn the head right side out. Make small holes at eye markings and insert the eyes. Embroider the nose and mouth onto the nose section. Stuff the head.

4. *To add the ears:* Sew a fabric ear to a fur ear, leaving the bottom open. Repeat for the other ear. Turn the ears right side out, fold the bottom raw edges in and hand stitch the ears in place on the top of the head.

5. *To make the tail:* Sew the base and end to the midsection of the tail; repeat for the other side. Sew the two halves together, leaving the end that will attach to the body open. Turn the tail right side out. Stuff lightly.

6. *To make the body:* Sew the front edges of the body fronts together. Sew the back edge of the body backs together, inserting the tail where indicated on the pattern. (Make sure to place the tail on the *inside* of the two body pieces so that it will be on the outside of the raccoon.) Sew the fronts to the backs at the side seams, leaving the neck edge open. Turn right side out.

7. *To make the arms:* Sew the paws to the inside arm pieces. Then stitch to the outside arm pieces, leaving the openings indicated on the pattern. Turn the arms right side out.

8. *To make the legs:* Sew pairs of leg pieces together, leaving the bottom and back openings indicated on the patterns. Clip where indicated. Sew the foot pads to the bottom of the legs, matching the dots on the pads with the seams. Turn the legs right side out.

9. *To assemble the raccoon:* Cut tiny slits at the Xs on the body, inside arms and inside legs. Sew four pairs of buttons together with strong thread, keeping the buttons about ¼ inch apart. Place the buttons inside each hole and connect the arms and legs to the body as shown at right.

10. *To finish the raccoon:* Stuff the body, arms and legs. Stitch the arm and leg openings closed. Sew the head to the body. Sew or glue small scraps of fur above the eyes for eyelashes.

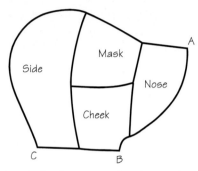

Sew the head pieces together, leaving the bottom open for stuffing.

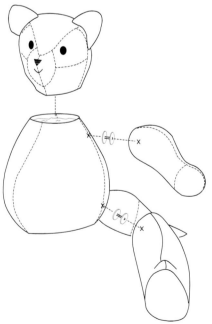

Stuffed Raccoon assembly.

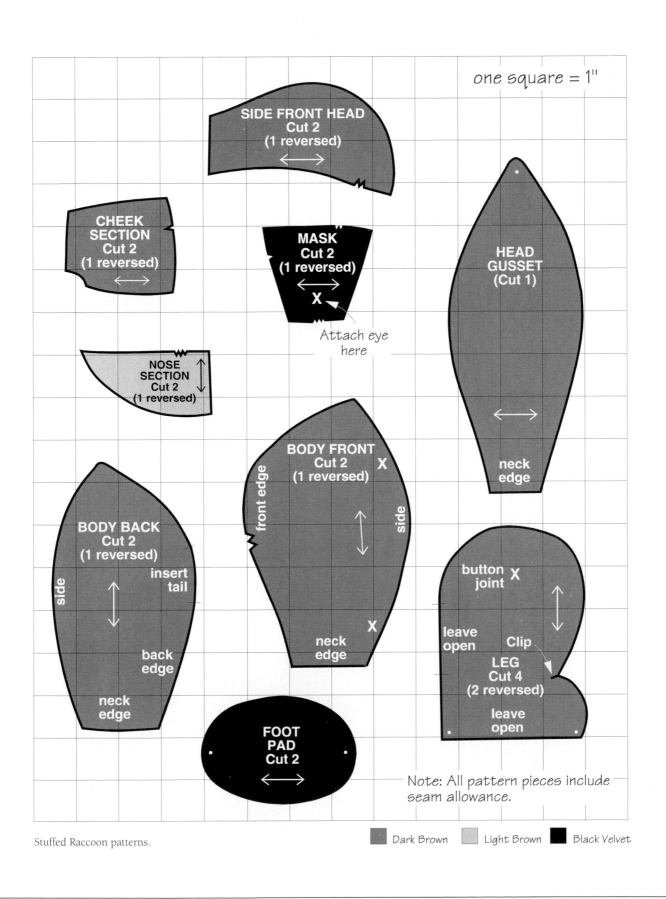

one square = 1"

SIDE FRONT HEAD
Cut 2
(1 reversed)

CHEEK
SECTION
Cut 2
(1 reversed)

MASK
Cut 2
(1 reversed)
X

Attach eye
here

HEAD
GUSSET
(Cut 1)

NOSE
SECTION
Cut 2
(1 reversed)

neck
edge

BODY FRONT
Cut 2
(1 reversed)
X

front edge

side

BODY BACK
Cut 2
(1 reversed)

insert
tail

side

back
edge

neck
edge

neck
edge

X

button
joint
X

leave
open

Clip

LEG
Cut 4
(2 reversed)

leave
open

FOOT
PAD
Cut 2

Note: All pattern pieces include
seam allowance.

Stuffed Raccoon patterns.

Dark Brown   Light Brown   Black Velvet

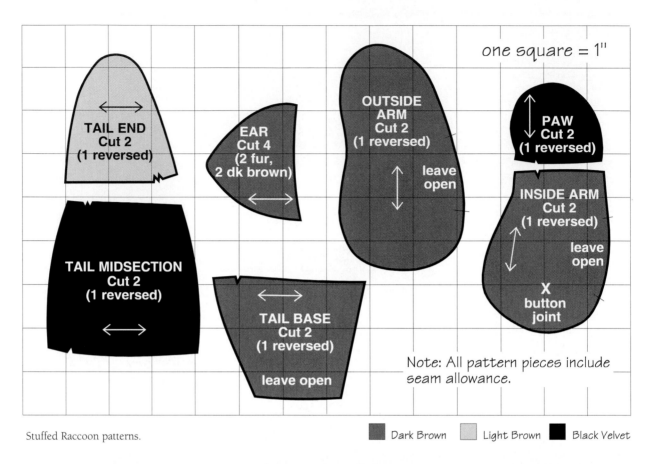

one square = 1"

TAIL END
Cut 2
(1 reversed)

EAR
Cut 4
(2 fur,
2 dk brown)

OUTSIDE
ARM
Cut 2
(1 reversed)

leave
open

PAW
Cut 2
(1 reversed)

INSIDE ARM
Cut 2
(1 reversed)

leave
open

X
button
joint

TAIL MIDSECTION
Cut 2
(1 reversed)

TAIL BASE
Cut 2
(1 reversed)

leave open

Note: All pattern pieces include seam allowance.

Stuffed Raccoon patterns.

| | Dark Brown | | Light Brown | | Black Velvet |

Braving the cold in Bethel, Maine.

KEEPSAKE WREATH

Beth Hylan, a wreath maker who lives in Wakefield, Massachusetts, combines her eye for antiques with her love of herbs when she creates her keepsake wreaths. Each wreath is a unique collection chosen especially for the recipient. You can include special family heirlooms or favorite treasures that the person already has (a favorite teacup, locket or small book) or you can search for appropriate keepsakes in attics and in secondhand stores. For baby wreaths such as this one, Beth looks for tiny old kid shoes, Victorian rattles, silver baby cups, brushes, combs and spoons. She also keeps an eye out for old linens and lace, bonnets, bibs or hankies.

1. Firmly attach a loop of sturdy wire on the top of the back of the wreath, so your hanger will be in place from the start.

2. Lay the wreath flat on a table or counter and begin to arrange the keepsakes on the bottom half of the wreath. You might want to play with the arrangement a bit before you begin to glue the keepsakes to

Materials

12–14" loosely woven grapevine wreath

3 or 4 treasures (tiny teacup, baby spoon, rattle, antique silver powder shaker)

Assorted ribbons, linens and lace

Assorted dried flowers and herbs (roses, delphinium, lavender, caspia, artemesia, sage and statice)

Glue gun

A Keepsake Wreath to celebrate a baby's birth—complete with cup and powder shaker.

the wreath. Beth recommends that you begin on the bottom half of the circle by draping a piece of linen or a lacy handkerchief from the inside of the circle to the outside edge. Let it hang gently over the outside. Then add keepsake items on top of that. When planning (before you glue), make sure the heaviest objects will be at the bottom of the wreath when it is finished.

3. When you have a fairly good idea of what you want it to look like, begin to glue, starting again with the linen or lacy hanky.

4. Arrange and glue the other trinkets, letting them gently overlap and cluster. Secure laces and linens by tucking them into the grapevines before you glue them. Use a lot of glue on big or heavy items. You can also use wire to secure items like a teacup or powder shaker, then camouflage the wire later with flowers, lace or ribbon.

5. When all the keepsakes have been attached, fill in the empty spaces by gluing on little bunches of dried flowers and herbs. Make sure you are generous with your dried material.

6. Finish the wreath with a bow made from old lace and ribbons (see "How to Tie a Beautiful Bow" on page 67).

ALMOST OLD LACE

If you can't find any nice old lace, you can buy new lace and let it soak briefly in cool tea until it has attained a mellow, antique look.

BASIC STENCILING TECHNIQUE

1. Make sure the surface you will be stenciling is clean and dry.

2. Make a full-size stencil pattern following instructions for "How to Enlarge a Pattern" on page 14.

3. Tape the pattern to a flat surface, then cover the pattern with a piece of Mylar, taping the edges to hold it in place. (If your design has more than one color, you will make a Mylar stencil for each color.) Trace the pattern onto the Mylar with a permanent felt-tip marker. To make a stencil for additional colors, remove the first sheet of Mylar (for color 1) and replace with a second sheet (for color 2). This time, you need to trace the cut-out area for color 2 and also trace "register marks," dotted lines that will help you position the stencil. Trace solid lines around the color 2 areas and dotted lines around the color 1 areas. Repeat for additional colors as needed.

4. Now you're ready to cut out the stencil patterns. Begin by placing each sheet of Mylar on a cutting mat or glass surface. Use a sharp X-Acto knife to follow the solid black lines; for smoothest cuts, turn the plastic as you go around corners or curves.

5. Tape your first stencil to the project you'll be working on.

6. Dip the tip of a stencil brush into your first color of paint. Apply the paint to the project, using circular strokes and moving from the edge of the stencil toward the middle. Always hold the brush perpendicular to the surface.

7. Gently lift the stencil, being careful not to smudge the paint. Allow the color to set until dry.

8. Tape the next stencil (for color 2) to the project using the dotted lines that you traced on the Mylar as register marks to help you position it. Make sure the dotted lines match the edges of the first color before you begin painting the second. Using a clean brush, apply the second color. Repeat until all the colors have been applied, letting the paint dry thoroughly between colors.

9. Clean the brushes and Mylar with soap and water.

CHRISTMAS SLED

Discarded sleds are easy to find at most yard sales, and the classic "Flexible Flyer" is a cheerful reminder of the headlong sledding of winters past. There are many ways to spruce up one of these classics. You can paint the sled as we have here, or you can refinish it by stripping, staining and varnishing it instead. The sled shown here comes from Nancy Walton, of Burlington, Massachusetts, from her collection of "101 Quick and Easy New England Crafts."

1. Prepare all wooden and metal surfaces by sanding off all flaking or cracked material and rust. (If necessary, use a wire brush to clean up the metal parts.)

2. Wipe all surfaces clean with mineral spirits.

3. When the surfaces are completely dry, prime the wood.

4. When the primer has dried, apply two coats of house paint, allowing the paint to dry thoroughly between coats.

5. Cover the wood near the metal parts with masking tape to protect it from paint splatters.

6. Apply two coats of rustproofing paint to all metal parts.

Materials

Wooden sled

Sandpaper, medium and fine

Rag

Mineral spirits

1 pint primer

1 pint acrylic exterior house paint

1 pint rustproofing paint

2" paintbrush (for wood)

1" paintbrush (for metal)

Masking tape

2 pieces (8½" × 11" each) of Mylar

X-Acto knife

Red, gold and green acrylic stencil paint

Stencil brush

Acrylic spray finisher (matte finish)

Using our pattern or your own, dress up an old attic find.

7. Remove the tape.

8. Enlarge the stencil patterns on the grid below, following the instructions in "How to Enlarge a Pattern" on page 14. (The other patterns are full size.) Transfer the stencil patterns to the Mylar sheets and cut them out. Refer to detailed instructions in "Basic Stenciling Technique" on page 36.

9. Tape the Mylar stencil to the sled, making sure it is centered. Position the stencils as shown in the photographs on page 37 and on the opposite page, or use your own arrangement.

10. Paint the stencil, and repeat the process as desired.

11. When it is completely dry, spray the stenciled area with matte finisher to protect it, especially if you plan to display the sled outdoors.

Stencil patterns for Christmas Sled.

one square = 1"

Fly like the wind on this stenciled sled.

Bright cardinals dress up your gifts.

CARDINAL GIFT TAGS

Neal Ward, an artist in Westford, Massachusetts, designed this easy stencil that anyone can make. You can cut up old Christmas cards or envelopes to make these handy gift tags. And if you enlarge the stencil following the instructions in "How to Enlarge a Pattern" on page 14, you can use the same pattern to make Christmas cards as well.

To get everyone involved, set up an "assembly line." One person can stencil-paint all the bodies, another can do the wings, and a third can work on the beaks and branches. Just make sure to clean the stencils often, since they're quite small and can easily become clogged with paint.

1. Trace the portions of the pattern shown as solid colors in Figures 1 through 3 onto each of the pieces of Mylar. As you trace the wing and beak/branch patterns, mark the outline of the cardinal (shown as a dotted line) to help with placement later.

2. Following the instructions in "Basic Stenciling Technique" on page 36, cut out the stencils.

Materials

8½" × 11" sheet of heavy paper or light cardboard

3 pieces (1½" × 2" each) of Mylar

Red and black fabric paint

4 yards narrow cranberry-colored ribbon, cut into 9" pieces

X-Acto knife

Figure 1   Figure 2   Figure 3   Stencil patterns for Cardinal Gift Tags.

3. Cut the paper or cardboard into 16 equal strips (Figure 4). The cardinal will be stenciled onto the *bottom* half of the strip.

4. Position the body pattern (Figure 1) slightly left of the center of the tag. Paint the body red. Allow the paint to dry, then position the wing pattern (Figure 2) so it slightly overlaps the body. (Use the dotted lines on the pattern to position the wing correctly.) This will make a darker red line where the body and wing meet.

5. After the red paint has dried completely, position the beak/branch pattern (Figure 3), using the dotted lines as a guide. Paint them with black paint. Let the paint dry completely.

6. Fold each strip in half lengthwise. Tie a length of ribbon around the fold in the card, and attach it to your package.

Note: The patterns are shown full-size.

Figure 4

Cut the paper into 16 equal strips, and stencil the cardinal on the bottom half of each strip.

SCENTED PILLOWS

Next time you're replacing your threadbare slipcovers and faded draperies, keep enough of the old fabric to make a few of Jan Flagg's small square and heart-shaped throw pillows. To make the pillow scented, just insert the sachet in the lapped back or the pocket. When you lean against the pillow or plump it under your head, you will release the fragrance.

Square Pillow

1. *To make the pillow:* Turn under 1 inch along one long side of each backing piece and press. Turn under again so the raw edges are not visible, and stitch in place. These overlapping pieces will form the lapped back for your pillow.

2. Keeping right sides together, align the long sides of the backing pieces with opposite sides of the front square. The backs will overlap. Sew around all four edges of the pillow, leaving a ½-inch opening at one corner. Trim the seam allowance at the corners and turn the pillow right side out.

3. Tuck one end of the cording into the opening in the seam. Hand tack the cording around the perimeter of the pillow. Tuck the other end into the opening and sew the seam closed. (If you are using lace for your trim, overlap the edges by ¼ inch and tack them together.) Insert the pillow form into the pillow through the lapped back. If you wish, you can attach small snaps or Velcro to close the lapped back.

4. *To make the sachet:* Place the two 5-inch squares one on top of the other. Sew a ⅝-inch seam around the perimeter, leaving a 2-inch opening. Turn the sachet right side out. Fill the sachet with your favorite sweet-smelling potpourri. Sew the opening closed, and place the sachet inside the pillow as shown at right.

Note: All seams are ⅝ inch.

Materials

13¼" square of tapestry material

2 pieces of backing material, 11¼" × 13¼"

50" of cording or other decorative trim

12" × 12" foam pillow form

Small snaps or Velcro (optional)

2 squares of muslin, 5" × 5"

Large handful of potpourri (your recipe or purchased at a gift store)

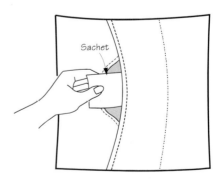

Insert the sachet into the lapped back of the Square Pillow.

Heart-Shaped Pillow

1. *To make the pillow:* Enlarge the heart pattern below using the instructions in "How to Enlarge a Pattern" on page 14 and transfer it to the tapestry and backing material. Cut out the hearts.

2. Press the edges of the 3½-inch square under ⅝ inch on all sides. Center and sew the square to the right side of the backing material, leaving the top open. This will form the pocket for your sachet.

3. Baste the lace to the tapestry, making sure that the straight edge of the lace is aligned with the raw edge of the fabric. Place the tapestry and backing material with right sides together. Sew around the perimeter of the heart, leaving a 2-inch opening on the side for turning and stuffing. Turn the pillow right side out.

4. Stuff the pillow firmly with fiberfill. Tuck one end of the cording into the seam opening, making sure that you can see it in front of the lace on the front of the pillow. Tack the cording around the perimeter of the heart, tucking the other end into the seam opening. Sew the opening closed.

5. *To make the sachet:* Place the two 2½-inch muslin squares one on top of the other. Sew a ⅝-inch seam around the perimeter, leaving one side open. Turn the sachet right side out and fill it with potpourri. Sew the opening closed, and place the sachet in its pocket.

Note: All seams are ⅝ inch.

Materials

8" square of tapestry material

8" square of backing material

3½" square of backing material

20" of 1½" wide lace

Polyester fiberfill

24" of satin cording

2 squares of muslin, 2½" × 2½"

Small handful of potpourri (your recipe or purchased at a gift store)

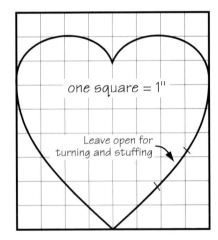

one square = 1"

Leave open for turning and stuffing

Heart-Shaped Pillow pattern.

Your guests will never suspect that these pretty pillows were made from old slipcovers.

CHAPTER FOUR

BASKETS TO MAKE AND FILL

decorative gifts for friends and neighbors

❧

Pe?ople the world over have been weaving baskets for centuries. It is a craft that has remained largely unchanged, despite industrial and political revolutions, space shuttles and computers. The best baskets are made by hand and made *for* hands—to hold, to carry, to fill with food, gifts, herbs and flowers.

As you no doubt remember from first grade, you can make a basket out of construction paper, an eggshell or a scooped-out lemon, as well as from woven reeds or tangled grapevines.

In this chapter you will find instructions for making baskets out of vines and lace, plus all you need to know to make a bread basket out of bread.

You will also find ideas for decorating and filling baskets. The graceful sleigh basket shown on page 53 and the mini bushel basket and the apple baskets shown on the opposite page were made by Downeaster Mary Skillings, who is a skilled weaver as well as a basket maker. Mary lives on an island in Harpswell, Maine. From her kitchen window, she can watch ospreys soaring over the shallow water as she sits and weaves baskets. Just as often, though, she steals time for basketmaking during one of her three children's soccer practices. Her baskets are always as beautiful as they are useful.

Whether you make your own baskets this season or find some as beautiful as Mary's, I hope they will all be fragrant and full of good surprises.

Fill your grapevine basket with herbs, gifts or goodies.

GRAPEVINE BASKET

Since New England is full of grapevines, it's no wonder we have such an abundance of grapevine wreaths and baskets. The basket here was made by Jennifer Plant, who lives on the border of Rhode Island and Massachusetts. (Jennifer learned the art of basket and wreath making from her mother, Irene Elizabeth Gray.) The basket shown here was filled and decorated by Elizabeth Timmins, an herb and flower designer who is Jennifer's neighbor. Although you may not have many of the herbs shown here, you can easily make your own substitutions. Or carry the basket to the next party you attend, filled with home-baked goodies.

1. Form a cylinder from the rectangle of wire. Place the square piece of wire underneath. Bend the corners of the square up and over the

Materials

4" × 18" piece of fencing wire

9" square of fencing wire

Brown rustproofing spray paint

Fresh, thin grapevines (must be pliable)

cylinder to hold the base to the sides. Spray the wire with the brown paint.

2. Remove all leaves from the vines. Begin weaving near the base. Wrap a vine loosely around the sides, threading it in and out of the wire. The "weave" can be quite loose—just go in and out of the wire enough to hold the vines to the side.

3. Attach a handle when you have woven halfway up the side. Tuck the bottom of the handle into the vines that have been woven, and secure the handle by weaving the vines over and under the handle as you finish the top half of the basket.

4. To make the basket bottom, weave the vines through the wire in a spiral, working from the outside to the inside.

5. Fill your basket.

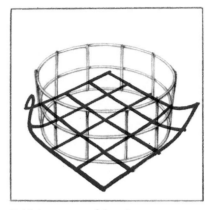

Fold the corners of the wire square up and over the cylinder to secure it.

Weave the vines loosely through the frame, beginning at the bottom.

Add the handle when you have woven halfway up the sides.

Weave the bottom in a spiral, beginning on the outside and working in.

Fill handmade baskets with seasonal items—apples, chestnuts, pinecones—to bring the outdoors inside.

Small crocheted doilies can be formed into cones and filled with tiny blossoms.

TINY TREE BASKETS

In our house we celebrate Advent as a penitential season. As a result, our children were not allowed candy during December until Christmas arrived. To make up for that, our Christmas trees were always laden with sweets—cookies, candied popcorn, candy canes and baskets full of Christmas candy. Some of our miniature tree baskets we picked up at the dime store. Others we made—from milkweed pods with ribbon handles, or halves of oranges, lemons or walnuts and even peach pits (see the photograph on page 45). We made cornucopias from lace doilies and paper.

Now, with only adult children, I have been filling the tree baskets with herbs, miniature hemlock cones and rosebuds. Sometimes I add a few tiny paper doves (page 24). And yes, I still fill one or two baskets with candy, just in case.

Lace Doily Basket

1. Cut the doily in half.

2. With the straight side as the bottom, fold the doily in thirds, shaping it into a cone and holding the third that overlaps between your thumb and fingers.

Materials
for Lace Doily Basket

5" round crocheted lace doily (available at craft stores)

White household glue

10" narrow satin ribbon

Handful of dried herbs and flowers

10" thin gold cord

Cut the doily in half and fold it into thirds.

Glue the overlapping edges securely.

Thread a ribbon through the doily and tie a small bow.

3. Generously spread glue on the adjoining surfaces of both overlapping pieces and hold the glued section together for a few minutes, until the glue holds quite securely.

4. When the glue is dry, thread the ribbon around the top, tying a small bow at the front.

5. Arrange and glue the flowers and herbs in the basket. Tie the gold thread on as a hanger, and hang the basket on your tree.

Mini Handle Basket

1. Choose an arrangement of flowers and herbs to go in the basket.

2. Apply glue to the bottom of each stem or flower and place it in the basket, holding it in place for a few minutes until the glue holds.

3. Tie the ribbon to the handle and hang your basket.

*Materials
for Mini Handle Basket*

Small (4–6") handle basket (available at craft stores)

Glue gun

Handful of dried herbs and flowers

12" narrow satin ribbon

Thumb-size Mini Handle Baskets, Straw Basket and Lemon Basket, filled with delicate gatherings.

Straw Basket

1. Stuff the basket firmly with the sponge or floral foam, making it slightly higher in the center.

2. Apply glue to the bottom of the tiny pinecones and place them very close together around the upper edge of the basket. Then fill in toward the center, again packing the cones in very closely.

3. Wrap the ribbon around the finished basket like a present, tying a bow at the top. Hang the basket with the streamers.

Lemon Basket

1. Spread a thick layer of glue on the inside of the lemon half.

2. Arrange the herbs and flowers inside the lemon half, pressing them firmly into the glue to make sure they stick.

3. Glue the ends of the twine inside the lemon, and hang it up.

Peach Pit Basket

1. Carefully flatten the bottom of the peach pit by cutting off the bottom as shown. Use a grinding wheel if you have one, or a sharp knife or small saw if you don't. Cut the handle into the peach pit.

2. Clean out the inside of the pit with a small, sharp knife.

3. Coat the inside of the basket with glue and fill it with the flowers.

Materials
for Straw Basket

Small (2" high) straw basket

Scrap of sponge or floral foam

24 tiny (1") pinecones

Glue gun

30" red-and-green ribbon

Materials
for Lemon Basket

½ lemon, with pulp scooped out and removed

Handful of dried herbs and flowers

Glue gun

6" piece of twine

Materials
for Peach Pit Basket

Fresh peach pit

White household glue

Handful of tiny flowers

At left, a children's gift basket with a ball, set of maracas, bag of marbles, seashell collection, book, game and magnifying glass. The hostess gift basket at right holds a bottle of wine and wine glass, flower water, scented soap, Balinese mask, jar of preserves, cheese and fresh fruit.

Flatten the bottom of the peach pit.

Cut the handle out of the sides.

These baskets are deliciously simple to make—and edible, too.

BREAD BASKET

A bread basket made and woven out of real bread dough is sure to become a conversation piece. But there's nothing particularly mysterious about making it—and anyone who likes to get his or her hands in dough will have a good time participating in the kneading, rolling, twisting and shaping. Let the sweet aroma of freshly baked bread welcome your guests. Then fill the basket with tiny rolls or breadsticks, and let it be the star of your holiday buffet. The recipe below will make one bread basket. If you want to make three dozen tiny rolls to go in the basket, just double the recipe.

1. *To make the dough:* Warm a large mixing bowl and measure the warm water into it. Sprinkle in the yeast and stir until it is completely dissolved.

2. Add the sugar, salt, butter and 3 cups of the flour. Beat with a wooden spoon until smooth. Add enough additional flour to make a stiff dough that holds its shape.

3. Turn the dough out onto a lightly floured board or countertop. Knead until smooth and elastic, about 8 to 10 minutes. Place the dough in a buttered bowl and turn it to thoroughly coat it with the butter. Cover the bowl with a damp cloth, and let the dough rise until doubled in bulk, about 1 hour.

4. *To make the bread basket:* Generously grease four strips of foil. Use them to cover the edges of a cooling rack, keeping the greased side up. Then grease the outside of a smooth-bottomed stainless steel mixing bowl and invert it onto the prepared rack.

Ingredients for Dough

2½ cups warm (110°) water

2 packages dry yeast

1 tablespoon sugar

1 tablespoon salt

2 tablespoons unsalted butter, softened

6½–7½ cups flour

1 egg, beaten

1 tablespoon milk

Materials for Bread Basket

Shortening

6 strips (2½" × 10" each) of aluminum foil

2 10" wire cooling racks

2 large stainless steel mixing bowls

Toothpicks

5. Punch the dough down and divide it into 24 equal pieces. Set 2 aside for the handle. To make the bottom of the basket, begin by rolling a piece of dough between your palms to form a 30-inch "rope." Make a second rope, then twist the two together. Wrap the twist around the bowl, beginning at the lower edge (the edge on the rack) and continuing up the side of the bowl. Make sure to leave no gaps. Make a second length of twisted rope the same way, pinch the end onto the end of the first rope, and continue winding and wrapping. Repeat until the bowl is completely covered.

6. Grease the additional foil and cover two opposite sides of the second cooling rack. Grease the other bowl and invert it onto the rack. Roll the two reserved pieces of dough into 24-inch ropes, twist them together, and place them *over* the bowl with the ends on the foil, as shown. This will form the basket handle.

7. Cover the basket and handle with slightly damp towels and let rise at room temperature until doubled in bulk, about 30 minutes.

8. Preheat the oven to 400°. Combine the egg and milk and brush the mixture gently on the basket and handle. Place the wire racks directly on the oven racks. Bake at 400° for 20 minutes (or until golden brown). Let the basket and the handle cool for about 10 minutes. Then remove from bowls and cool on wire racks. When the basket section is cool, turn it right side up.

9. To attach the handle, insert toothpicks into each end of the handle, then into the upper edges of the basket. Gently lower the handle into position on the basket, using the toothpicks to hold it in place.

10. *To make the tiny rolls:* Use the same recipe as for the bread basket. Pull off a 1-inch ball of dough. Roll it into a 6-inch rope. Tie it in a knot. Repeat until the dough is used up. Let the knots rise at room temperature for 30 minutes, then bake at 400° for 15 minutes or until golden brown. Fill the basket with the rolls for a beautiful, edible centerpiece.

Wrap the twisted strands of dough around a greased, inverted bowl, beginning at the bottom and working your way up.

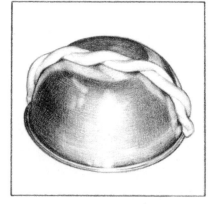

Form the handle from one twisted rope placed over an inverted bowl.

Attach the handle to the basket with toothpicks.

LAVENDER-COVERED BASKET

If you have a lot of dried lavender blossoms, you can make the basket shown at the beginning of this chapter (on page 44). I used a small basket to make this beautiful, freshly scented present, but you can also use a miniature flower pot.

1. Coat the outside of the basket liberally with glue.

2. Roll the basket in the loose lavender blossoms until it is thickly covered. Let it dry.

3. Tightly pack the basket with foam, leaving ½ to 1 inch of space around the top for the sheet moss.

4. Cut moss to fit over the foam and glue it on.

5. Cut all the lavender stalks to the same height (make sure they will fit underneath the handle). Carefully poke them into the moss and the foam, in a fairly close bunch in the center of the basket.

6. Embellish with a bow if you like.

Materials

Small (6" diameter) handle basket

White household glue

½–¾ cup loose lavender blossoms, depending on size of container

Floral foam

Sheet moss

20 to 40 lavender stalks with blossoms, depending on size of container

Ribbon (optional)

Look for baskets that fit the gift—Santa's sleigh can deliver your gift of chocolates.

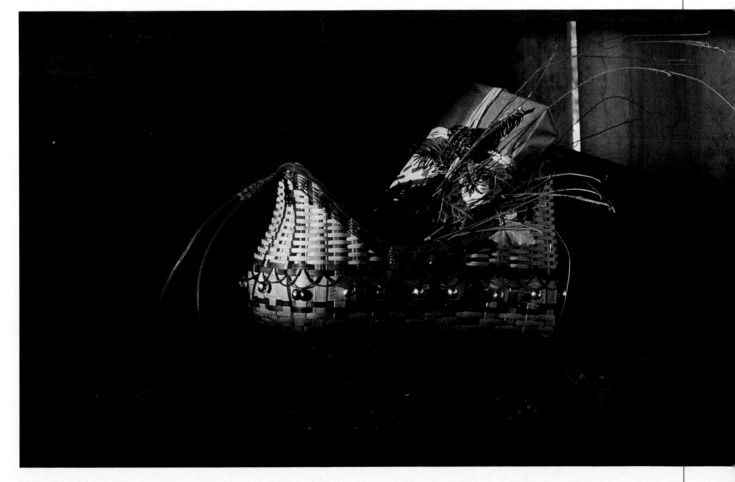

CHAPTER FIVE

DECORATIONS
FROM
NATURAL MATERIALS

crafts from forest and field

T he part of preparing for Christmas that I look forward to the most is when I go into the woods and fill my basket with pinecones, bits of emerald moss and fresh greens. Remember, December is the ideal month for pruning laurels and rhododendrons, and you can then combine those glossy leaves with feathery evergreens when you're making wreaths and garlands.

Right after Thanksgiving, in come all the sand dollars and sun-bleached shells I gathered last August at low tide. I take down bunches of herbs and sea lavender from the beams in my study where they've been drying upside down. I buy a lot of fresh walnuts from my grocery store around Thanksgiving—some to eat and more to paint for my tree.

Oranges and flu are both making their annual appearance, too, and I keep a good supply of the former on hand in an attempt to stave off the latter. If you save your orange peels the way I do, and dry them (I do it in the microwave), you will be halfway to a potpourri. Which reminds me to ask the dairy man at the market to save the next round wooden box that big wheels of cheese come in. After a thorough airing, these make great containers for large amounts of potpourri, Christmas sweets or other presents.

Opening wide off our kitchen is a little sunken room with small, irregular windows, still called the teamster's room from long ago when the man who drove the farm team actually lived there. I use it as my Christmas room and set up the card table in front of my big, faded wing chair. This room is where I spread everything out, where I stash presents, and finally, where we set up the tree. The teamster's room is warm and smells of wood smoke, ginger-bread and potpourri. From my chair I can see the chickadees and cardinals bickering for perches at the feeder, and in the open field beyond, shaggy horses prod the snow with sharp hooves, hoping to find a few green sprigs underneath. I sometimes wish I could stay here forever, and that it would always be just a week or two 'til Christmas.

WALNUT STRAWBERRIES

The first Christmas that herbalist Elizabeth Timmins cele-brated as a young wife, she decorated her tree with these walnut "strawberries" and nothing else. When she describes the tree now, more than a dozen years later, from Hidden Brook Herbs in North Dighton, Massachusetts, her voice is wistful and her eyes shine. It's a surprise to find strawberries on a Christmas tree—but somehow they always look just right. I like to use a high-gloss paint that catches the reflec-tion of the Christmas tree lights.

Materials

Walnuts

Red craft paint (high-gloss)

Paintbrush (unless you use spray paint)

White craft paint (not spray)

Toothpicks

Gold cord or thick thread

Glue gun or white household glue

Green felt

1. Cover a walnut with red paint.

2. When the paint is dry, dot it with specks of white paint for seeds. Your walnut-in-disguise looks more like a strawberry if you have a thicker concentration of seeds at the bottom of the walnut and fewer at the top. (I find that I can make better dots using a toothpick rather than a tiny paintbrush.)

3. Cut a 6-inch length of cord and double it over. Glue the loose ends onto the walnut as a hanging loop.

4. Transfer the leaf pattern from the opposite page onto the felt, one for each strawberry. (Or cut them out freehand if you are more skilled than I.) Cut a slit from the edge to the center of the leaf, and glue it around the base of the loop.

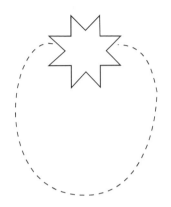

Walnut Strawberry leaf pattern.

Perhaps not a traditional Christmas decoration—but these strawberries will brighten any tree.

PRESSED FLOWER ORNAMENTS

These ornaments are easy to make and look elegant hanging on your tree or in a window with the light coming through. I always try to press a few little flowers in the summer—johnny jump-ups, small wild asters and flowering herbs. But even in the fall you can usually find some lacy leaves and grasses to press for a day or two. Or, you could buy fresh baby's breath, asters or other small blossoms from the florist.

1. Make sure the slides are clean.

2. Arrange a flower or two on a slide.

3. When the arrangement is the way you want it, carefully glue it onto the slide, using as little glue as possible.

4. Make a loop with the gold thread and glue the loose ends to the center of the top edge of the slide.

5. Put a drop of glue on each corner of the slide, one on the loop (on top of the end that you have already glued to the bottom slide), and one in the middle of each of the two long sides.

6. Carefully place another slide on top, so the edges all match. Hold it in place for a minute or two, until the glue has set.

Materials

Microscope slides, glass or Plexiglas

Assorted small pressed flowers and leaves

Clear-drying glue

Gold thread or transparent fishing line

Loop of thread

Dots of glue

Dried Flowers

Use clear glue to secure the slides together.

PASTRY-TIN ORNAMENT

Madeleine DiCicco, an herbal designer for Crabtree & Evelyn and teacher of herbal crafts from Burlington, Massachusetts, is a genius for putting flowers in the least-expected spots, such as a tiny pastry tin. This is a twinkly little ornament, and it may give you ideas for variations. For instance, you can also use small, shiny cookie cutters, gluing the flowers on the inside of the rim.

1. Glue whatever catches your fancy on the inside of the tin, making sure the inside is completely covered. (Remember, the tin will be hanging so that the bottom will be seen and the contents will show.)

2. Make a loop of ribbon and tie a nice little bow at the end.

3. Glue the bow onto the upper edge of the tin.

Materials

Tiny (2") pastry tin

Glue gun

Assorted dried flowers, herbs, rose hips or pepper berries, tiny hemlock cones or oak moss

20" narrow satin ribbon

Fill shiny pastry tins with seasonal greens, flowers and pinecones.

OPEN YOUR CONES

If your pinecones haven't completely opened, put them on a foil-covered cookie sheet in a 250°–275° oven. Watch them carefully. The heat will cause them to open, and they will release fragrant sap, making your whole house smell like Christmas.

Treasured miniature wreaths to hang on your tree.

MINI PINECONE WREATH

I learned about these little wreaths from Susan Bates who raises herbs and sheep in Townsend, Massachusetts. This one is made with the smallest pinecones available. Here in Bedford, Massachusetts, I use hemlock or larch cones. The number you need will depend on the sizes of the cones and the ring you use as a base. When I use a 3-inch ring as a base, I can usually fit 22 to 30 tiny cones around the ring.

1. Glue 5 or 6 pinecones on the inside of the ring, pointing toward the center. The base of each cone should just touch the cones on either side.

2. Glue about 8 to 11 cones around the face of the ring, tops pointing almost straight up, with just a little tilt to the outside. Again, the bases should touch.

3. Glue approximately 10 to 14 cones around the outside of the ring, cones pointing out and bases touching one another.

4. Form a loop out of the ribbon and tie with a nice, small bow. Glue the bow securely to the upper part of the ring, near the center, and hang from your tree.

Materials
30 small pinecones
3" diameter craft ring
20" narrow ribbon
Glue gun

Glue tiny pinecones to the inside (1), face (2) and outside (3) of the ring.

FIRE-STARTER PINECONES

These are good presents for children to make, but only if someone is there to supervise melting the wax. You can use any medium to large cone as a base. It can be covered by any kind of wax—simple paraffin, paraffin colored by adding a few pieces of crayon, or melted-down candle stumps.

Materials

Pinecones

Wax (paraffin, old candles, crayons)

Small muffin tins or votive candle holders

Cooking oil

Household string

1. Melt the wax in a double boiler over low heat, being careful that it doesn't get too hot and ignite.

2. Oil the muffin tins or candle holders.

3. Pour about ½ inch of melted wax into the bottom of the tins or holders.

4. Let the wax cool and harden.

5. Cut a 3-inch wick from the string.

6. Lay one end of the wick across the wax in the tin and let the other end hang out of the side of the tin.

7. Stand the pinecone up in the tin on top of the wick.

8. Pour another ½ inch of melted wax around the base of the cone and let it harden.

9. When the wax is completely hard, remove the cones from the tins. (The flat wax base, along with the wick, should lift out of the tin when you remove the cone.)

Place one of these cones among your firewood, and light the wick for a merrily blazing fire.

Add a taste of cinnamon to any hot drink—and let Santa keep you company.

CINNAMON STICK SANTAS

This is a perfect project for young children, since you only need a few long cinnamon sticks and some craft paint. And if they "mess up" one Santa's face, they can always paint another. I like to see a few Santas hanging on the tree, but they make great gifts as well. Just tuck them into a gift basket with a new mug, some good cocoa powder and a plump pouch of cookies.

1. With a small paintbrush, paint a Santa face on one end of the cinnamon sticks. For the cheeks, I just mix a little red paint into white to make pink. (Of course, the other way is just to buy pink paint.) Using a sponge instead of a brush will give a nice, curly texture to the beard.

2. When the paint has dried, tie three sticks together with a pretty ribbon.

Materials

Cinnamon sticks, at least 6" long

White, red, pink (optional) and blue or black craft paint

Small paintbrush

Sponge (optional)

Ribbon

BAY LEAF POTPOURRI

Madeleine DiCicco of Burlington, Massachusetts, makes up great quantities of this spicy mixture and keeps it in a tightly sealed plastic bag both to preserve the scent and to prevent any insects from flying in. Dry the orange peel before adding it to the potpourri. For a quick-drying technique, place the orange peel on a paper towel in your microwave, set on high for 3 minutes. (Repeat as necessary until the peels are completely dry.) The slower method is to leave the peels out on a wire rack or hanging from a line for two to three weeks. By then, they should be dry enough to add to the mix.

1. Use equal parts cinnamon sticks, allspice, bay leaves and orange peel. Roughly crush the cinnamon and allspice (Madeleine stamps on hers), and mix with the bay and orange peel.

2. Add a few drops of oil of cinnamon and mix together. I usually wait a little while, leave the room and return to check the fragrance. Remember, you can always add more oil, but you can't take any away, so be judicious.

3. When the mixture satisfies your nose, add orrisroot, about 1 table-spoon per cup of potpourri. Let it ripen in a tightly closed bag for a week or two.

Materials
Cinnamon sticks
Allspice, whole
Bay leaves
Orange peel, dried
Oil of cinnamon
Orrisroot, ground or crushed

This potpourri gives a spicy fragrance to your holiday home.

Adorn this Twig Tree with gumdrops or more traditional ornaments.

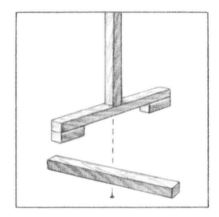

Nail the stand pieces together.

TWIGS OF CHRISTMAS

Happy was the day I stumbled upon Clint Flagg in his secret garden on Cape Cod. Clint has the eyes and hands of a true artist and the nimble, generous spirit of a child. He invented the bare-branched tree shown here. Yankees have a unique affinity for these sparse little trees—all winter long we view stark, bare branches against gray skies.

1. Nail the 24-inch piece of wood (the "trunk" of the tree) upright onto the center of one of the 9-inch pieces, as shown above. Nail the two short pieces to the underside, at either end, to serve as supports. Then nail the remaining 9-inch piece perpendicular to the first 9-inch piece. This forms your stand.

2. Cut the branches into twigs, varying the lengths from about 1 inch to about 8 inches. You will need several dozen twigs.

3. Nail the branches to the trunk, beginning at the bottom with the longest twigs and ending at the top with the shortest ones.

4. When all the branches are nailed in place, take the pruning shears and prune it into shape.

Variation: For a half-round tree, leave one whole side, from top to bottom, free of branches. The half-round trees are perfect for mounting on walls or doors.

Nail the twigs to the trunk, beginning at the bottom with the longest ones.

Materials

1 piece wood, 1" × 1" × 24"

2 pieces wood, 1" × 1" × 9"

2 pieces wood, 1" × 1" × 2½"

Approximately 10 large maple branches

Pruning shears

Small nails

Hammer

BAY LEAF GARLAND

Beth Hylan, owner of Sweetbay, an herbal shop in Wakefield, Massachusetts, assures me her garlands are a snap to make. Bay leaves are the "basics," but Beth makes many variations, some with dried peppers and corn husks, some with dried pomegranates and orange slices and this one with cinnamon sticks and dried apple slices. The best place to get bay leaves in quantity, according to Beth, is from a craft shop or dried flower store.

1. Drill holes through the centers of the cinnamon sticks. Thread the twine through the needle and tie one end in a large knot.

2. Thread two cinnamon sticks and pull twine through. Then carefully thread on bay leaves, five or six at a time, until you have 2 inches of leaves.

3. String on a cinnamon stick and then another 2 inches of bay leaves. Add one or two dried apple slices followed by 2 inches of bay leaves.

4. Continue this pattern until you have just enough twine left to make another good anchoring knot, ending, if possible, with two cinnamon sticks.

5. Tie raffia bows onto the garland near the cinnamon sticks.

Materials

Cinnamon sticks
Dried apple slices
½ pound whole bay leaves
36" piece of twine
Large-eye needle (big enough to thread the twine)
Red raffia

Alternate bay leaves with apple slices and cinnamon sticks until your garland is complete.

SWEET BAY RING

Here's another fragrant holiday decoration from Beth Hylan. It's a solid garland of bay leaves formed into a ring, hung with raffia and accented with cinnamon sticks and dried flowers. At Christmas I like to hang one of these rings in the doorway so every time I walk beneath it, I smell the cinnamon and bay leaves.

1. Gently string the bay leaves through the center directly onto the wire, packing them closely together. Leave ¾ inch of wire at each end.

Materials

About ⅓ pound whole bay leaves
12" heavy wire
Pliers
Red raffia
Cinnamon sticks
Dried flowers

2. Form a ring by joining the ends of the wire together and twisting them tightly. Using the pliers, fold the wire over and form it into a flat edge.

3. With the raffia, make a loop for a hanger, and then tie the ends into a nice loop bow that will gently lie over the bay leaves.

4. Decorate the top of the bow by gluing on a few cinnamon sticks and dried flowers.

After stringing the bay leaves, form a ring.

Dress up your house with a decorative and fragrant bay ring and garland.

SEA LAVENDER BALL

Clint and Jan Flagg say that this ball (shown on page 54) reminds them of how small our world is and how simple it is to find beauty in it. You can spray the orb lightly with gold to give it a shine, or leave it the humble way it comes, covered with sprigs of sea lavender. Although sea lavender shares its name with the more common form of lavender, it comes from a different family of plants and is also known as statice.

1. Insert wire all the way through the center of the Styrofoam ball. Put a twist in the wire and form a flat loop across the bottom. (This will prevent the wire from pulling out.) Make a small loop at the top of the wire to form a hanger.

2. Cut off 4-inch sprays of sea lavender and insert them about an inch into the ball until the ball is completely covered and no Styrofoam shows.

3. If you want to paint the ball gold, spray it now and let the paint dry thoroughly before proceeding.

4. Glue on the rosebuds, mixing them at random with the lavender.

5. Tie on a bow and add the shells under it. Follow the instructions in "How to Tie a Beautiful Bow" on the opposite page, if you like.

6. Hang it from the wire loop with more ribbon or gold thread.

Materials

4" diameter Styrofoam ball

7" florist's wire

1 big bunch sea lavender (available at craft shops)

Gold spray paint (optional)

12 small rosebuds

Glue gun

4 yards pink or burgundy silk or satin wired ribbon with gold edges

Seashells

Gold thread or extra ribbon

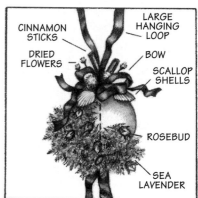

Attach the sea lavender to the ball first, then add rosebuds and seashells.

A winter evening is lit up by the Nubble lighthouse in York, Maine.

HOW TO TIE A BEAUTIFUL BOW

You will need three lengths of double-faced satin ribbon: $4^5/_8 \times$ 25 inches; $4^5/_8 \times$ 50 inches; and $^3/_4 \times$ 10 inches. You will also need two 5-inch pieces of florist's wire.

1. Lay the 25-inch piece of ribbon flat, then bring the ends in and overlap them slightly (Figure 1). Pinch the center and tie securely with a short piece of florist's wire (Figure 2).

2. Find the center of the 50-inch piece of ribbon and form a loop in the center that matches the size of the loops in the shorter piece. Tie a short piece of florist's wire to secure this loop also (Figure 3).

3. Place the short bow across and on top of the long one (Figure 4). Crisscross the narrow ribbon around the bows as shown. Pull the ribbon tight, tie a knot in the back and trim the ends.

Christmas Eve finds small children throughout New England waiting for Santa.

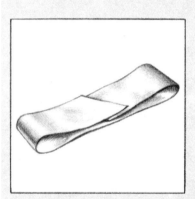

Figure 1. Overlap the ends of the short piece of ribbon.

Figure 2. Tie the center with wire.

Figure 3. Form a loop in the long piece of ribbon and tie it with wire.

Figure 4. Place the long piece on top of the short piece. Tie the narrow ribbon around the loops and secure in the back.

CHAPTER SIX

THREE FESTIVE MENUS

holiday meals to prepare and share

☙

*T*he high points of our long New England winters are those feasts we have around Christmas time. We come together to celebrate our friendship, our kinship, our intertwined lives, our good fortune in having food, light, warmth and each other.

Here in New England, we need happy gatherings to counteract our short, gray days and penetrating damp chill. We need parties that allow us to come closer around a warm, welcoming hearth and share a cup of wassail.

In this chapter are menus for three different kinds of feasts—an informal winter party to follow an afternoon of skating, skiing or perhaps sleigh riding; a Christmas dinner; and a holiday buffet for all ages.

INFORMAL WINTERFEST

❧

JACKSON HOUSE CREAM CHEESE AND
PEPPER JELLY TOAST
OLD MOSES FARM BEEF STEW IN RED WINE
WOODSTOCK BUBEN SPAETZLE
ROSEMARY COUNTRY BREAD (PAGE 6)
GLAZED CARROTS AND SHALLOTS
ALMOND ANGEL CAKE WITH ALMOND CREAM
WOODSTOCK SPICED WASSAIL

INFORMAL WINTERFEST

In New England we celebrate ice and snow by heading outdoors as soon as possible. What I look forward to the most are those rare nights of smooth ice, snowy fields and enough moonlight to skate by.

In a world as cold and sparkling as the snow scene from "The Nutcracker," we skim across the glassy pond, weightless and free. The Concord River flows just beyond the meadows and, even though the children have grown up and moved on, my husband, Upton, and I still wait for the river to freeze so we can fly on skates or skis from Bedford north to Billerica, or south to the Great Meadows Wildlife Refuge. We call our friends and get the stew going.

Here is a menu designed to complete a skating party or a sleigh ride, to celebrate a blizzard or rekindle winter-weary friendships. So get out your skates and sled, your pots and platters, and enjoy!

JACKSON HOUSE CREAM CHEESE AND PEPPER JELLY TOAST

Elegant Jackson House in Woodstock, Vermont, welcomes sleigh riders and cross-country skiers to its late-afternoon high tea. Here you can warm up and relax in an armchair in front of the snapping fire and settle in with a cup of hot tea accompanied by treats such as these Pepper Jelly Toasts. The recipe calls for jalapeño peppers, but if they are too hot for you, try making the jelly with milder chili peppers. For best results, chop the peppers in your blender or food processor.

To make the jelly: In a large, nonaluminum saucepan, combine the peppers, vinegar and pectin. (If you use jalapeño peppers, you should wear rubber gloves to protect your hands.) Bring to a boil, stirring, to dissolve the pectin. Add the sugar all at once. Return to a full, rolling boil. Boil for 5 minutes. Add 1 or 2 drops of green or red food coloring to make the jelly more colorful. Pour into sterilized jars as you would for any jelly and seal properly while hot.

To make the toast: Lightly toast the bread, then cut into festive shapes (cookie cutters work well for this). Spread with a layer of cream cheese, then add the pepper jelly on top.

An added bonus—this recipe makes enough jelly so there's some left over to use as a meat relish, to spread on crackers and eat after the guests have gone home.

Makes 6 cups.

Jelly

6	cups (approximately 8 peppers) finely chopped and seeded bell peppers, red or green, including their juice
1	cup finely chopped jalapeño or chili peppers, red or green to match bell peppers
4	cups white vinegar
2	packages pectin
12	cups sugar
	Green or red food coloring

Toast

1	loaf fresh white bread, sliced thin
8	ounces cream cheese, softened

A single illuminated church steeple lights the way home for residents of East Corinth, Massachusetts.

OLD MOSES FARM BEEF STEW IN RED WINE

To me, there is no meal more satisfying than stew. And this recipe is a hearty one—a generous serving will fill the empty stomach of even the most vigorous skater. The recipe is adapted from one shared by the Old Moses Farm in South Strafford, Vermont, and was originally a venison stew. This beef version is a robust winner, as you will find out by the way your kitchen smells while the stew simmers quietly on the back of the stove. Make it ahead and keep it refrigerated until you warm and serve it.

To make the stew: Heat the oil in a large, heavy-bottomed pot over medium-high heat. Season the beef with salt and pepper and brown it, one-third at a time, on all sides. Remove the beef from the pan with a slotted spoon and set aside. When all the beef has been browned and removed, turn the heat down to medium and fry the bacon for a few minutes, until crisp. Add the thyme, bay leaves, tomato paste and flour. Stir constantly and cook for a few more minutes, until well blended and browned so the flour doesn't taste raw.

Deglaze the pan with the vinegar and wine by pouring them into the pan and using a wooden spoon to scrape the solid bits off the bottom. When the alcohol has burned off, add the stock and the beef, with its juices, to the pan and bring just to a boil. Turn the heat down, cover the stew and let it simmer for a couple of hours, until the beef is tender. Stir it from time to time, and add water if it looks too dry. When the meat is cooked, add the onions and mushrooms, and adjust the seasoning if necessary. Remove the bay leaves. Serve the stew with Buben Spaetzle and Glazed Carrots and Shallots (opposite page). Garnish with a few leafy watercress sprigs, and serve the jelly on the side so each guest can stir a spoonful into their serving.

Variations: You can augment this stew by garnishing with herbs just before serving. If you have some fresh or dried basil on hand, chop it up with some fresh Italian parsley and sprinkle it over each serving.

To make a venison stew, use 3 pounds of venison stew meat and substitute the game stock on page 86 for the beef stock. Add 10 crushed juniper berries with the herbs.

Makes 8 servings.

5	tablespoons olive oil
3	pounds beef stew meat, cut into bite-size pieces
	Salt and freshly ground pepper to taste
4	slices bacon, cut crosswise into small strips
1	teaspoon thyme
2	bay leaves
2	tablespoons tomato paste
4	tablespoons flour
2	tablespoons red wine vinegar
1	cup dry red wine
1	cup beef stock
½	pint pearl onions
½	pound mushrooms, quartered
	Watercress sprigs (optional)
3	tablespoons apple cider jelly or currant jelly

WOODSTOCK BUBEN SPAETZLE

A traditional Swiss dish, this version is a delicious amalgam of potatoes, flour and seasonings, similar to potato dumplings or gnocchi. It is an appropriate accompaniment to any stew. The dough is easy to make and, like the stew, can be cooked a few days ahead and kept in the refrigerator. At the last moment, lightly brown the spaetzle and serve.

2	pounds potatoes, cooked and mashed
2	cups flour
4	eggs
½	teaspoon salt (or to taste)
¼	teaspoon freshly ground pepper
¼	teaspoon freshly grated nutmeg
9	tablespoons butter

Combine all the ingredients except 5 tablespoons of the butter in a large bowl and mix thoroughly. Chill the mixture well. Take small pieces of the spaetzle dough and roll between the palms of your hands into little twigs. (This is a great job for children, who call the spaetzle worms, not twigs.)

Fill a large pot with salted water and bring to a rolling boil. Add the spaetzle. When it is done (approximately 4 to 5 minutes), the spaetzle will float to the top and will be tender yet firm to the bite. Drain off the water carefully, and gently toss the spaetzle with 4 tablespoons of butter. (You may cover and refrigerate the spaetzle at this point.)

To prepare for serving, put 1 tablespoon of butter in a large skillet and melt over medium-high heat. When the foam begins to subside, toss in the spaetzle and brown it lightly. Season, if necessary, with additional salt and pepper.

Makes 8 servings.

GLAZED CARROTS AND SHALLOTS

Even the most finicky eater won't be able to resist these buttery, shiny carrots. And they make a colorful addition to any meal. My favorite part about making this dish is that the vegetables simmer so beautifully by themselves on the back burner while I am busying myself with the final preparations for the meal.

12	carrots, cut into julienne sticks
1	cup ginger ale
4	tablespoons butter
24	shallots
½	cup red wine
	Chicken stock as needed
	Parsley (optional)

Cook the carrots, partially covered, over very low heat in a small amount of ginger ale and 2 tablespoons of butter, replenishing the ginger ale as it evaporates from the pan.

Cook the shallots, partially covered, over very low heat in 2 tablespoons of butter and the wine, adding chicken stock from time to time as the liquid evaporates.

Remove the vegetables from the heat as soon as they are tender and the liquid is reduced to a syrupy glaze—about 35 to 40 minutes for the carrots; longer for the shallots. Combine in a serving dish and garnish with a little parsley. Serve while still warm.

Makes 8 servings.

ALMOND CREAM

This resembles Crème Anglais but has far fewer calories. It is superb with the Almond Angel Cake that follows.

6	egg yolks
5	tablespoons sugar
1/4	teaspoon salt
1 1/2	cups milk
3/4	teaspoon vanilla
1/8	teaspoon almond extract

Whisk together the egg yolks, sugar and salt in a large, nonaluminum saucepan. In a separate saucepan, scald the milk. While beating the egg mixture, gradually add the (still hot) scalded milk. Over medium heat, stir the custard constantly with a metal spoon for 3 to 4 minutes, or until custard coats the spoon. Place custard in a cool bowl and stir in the vanilla and almond extract. Cover the bowl and refrigerate until serving.

Makes 1 1/2 cups.

ALMOND ANGEL CAKE

I always like to have an angel cake at Christmas (for all the angels, of course) and this one is a honey because it is very low in calories and fat.

3/4	cup almonds, finely ground to flour
9	tablespoons flour, sifted
3	tablespoons cornstarch
1	cup sugar
14	egg whites (at room temperature)
1	teaspoon vanilla
1/2	teaspoon almond extract
1/8	teaspoon salt
1/2	teaspoon cream of tartar

Preheat the oven to 350°. Wash and dry thoroughly a 9-inch tube pan. In a small bowl, sift together the almond flour, flour, cornstarch and 2 tablespoons of the sugar.

In a large bowl, beat the egg whites with the vanilla and almond extract, using an electric mixer set on low speed, until foamy. Add the salt and cream of tartar and continue beating at medium speed until the meringue forms soft peaks. Increase the speed to high and, adding the remaining sugar 1 teaspoon at a time, continue beating until the mixture is stiff but not dry. With a rubber spatula, gently fold the flour and sugar mixture into the meringue.

Use a rubber spatula to spread the meringue inside the cake pan. Run a very thin-bladed knife or a skewer through the batter to release any large air pockets. Bake in the center of a 350° oven for 35 to 40 minutes or until golden brown. Remove from the oven and place upside down on a wire rack to cool for 1 hour.

Run a thin-bladed knife around both sides of cake to loosen it, then invert the pan again. The cake will eventually come right out. Cool completely on rack before serving. Serve slices with dollops of Almond Cream on top.

Makes 8 servings.

A fence winds its way across a field in Burke, Vermont.

The perfect winter drink from Woodstock, Vermont.

WOODSTOCK SPICED WASSAIL

This winter libation from the Woodstock Inn in Woodstock, Vermont (see page 101), will warm you from head to toe. You might even want to cut up the apples and take some wassail with you in a thermos to the frozen pond, or tuck a thermosful under the seat in the sleigh.

 Core the apples, peel a ring off the tops and place in a small baking dish. In a heavy saucepan, combine the sugar and brandy, bring to a boil and pour over the apples. Cover the baking dish and bake the apples at 350° until they are soft, about 30 minutes. Combine the water, cinnamon, cloves, allspice, wine and sherry in a large nonaluminum pot and bring to a boil. Simmer for 10 minutes. Put the apples in a heatproof punch bowl with their juices and pour the hot mulled wine over them. Strain out the cloves, if desired.

Makes about ½ gallon.

6	small baking apples
1	cup brown sugar
1	cup brandy
1	cup water
4–5	broken cinnamon sticks
1	teaspoon whole cloves
1	teaspoon allspice
1	liter red wine
1⅔	cups dry sherry

CHRISTMAS DINNER

LEMON-GARLIC CHRISTMAS OLIVES
CHEDDAR CROQUETTES WITH TOMATO CHUTNEY
ROAST LOIN OF PORK WITH PRUNES AND APPLES
CIDER SAUCE
RED POTATOES BAKED IN PARCHMENT
ROOT VEGETABLES ROASTED WITH SAGE AND THYME
NEWPORT CHRISTMAS PLUM PUDDING (PAGE 10)
HARD SAUCE (PAGE 10)
BRANDY SAUCE (PAGE 10)
CHAMPAGNE

Choosing the family Christmas tree in Shelburne, Vermont.

CHRISTMAS DINNER

Traditional as a family Christmas dinner may seem to us now, many New England household, right into the early part of this century, did not have Christmas dinner or even Christmas trees in their own homes. Instead, families gathered around the enormous tree in the community hall or church, many voices caroling together, the children eager to receive their single present and a cornucopia of candy. All the women pitched in, bringing their favorite dishes to make a feast worthy of a king.

People in rural New England a century ago were as removed from their neighbors by miles as we are today by our demanding schedules. A community Christmas gave grown-ups a chance to catch up with each other while the children cavorted in a noisy and probably naughty pack.

Maybe we should go back to this communal way of celebrating, especially in a society where more of us work away from our homes and fewer of us have families nearby. The idea of an extended family feast where no one has to do it all? Well, think about it as you prepare your own Christmas dinner. And if it's this one you're making, remember, it only serves six.

Except for the Plum Pudding (page 10) and the Christmas Olives, all the recipes come from Simon Pearce, who has a restaurant and pottery and glass workshop in Quechee, Vermont (see page 102).

ROOT VEGETABLES ROASTED WITH SAGE AND THYME

Cut an assortment of peeled root vegetables— carrots, onions, parsnips, turnips, rutabagas and salsify—into julienne strips about 2 inches long and ¼ inch square. Slice some celery and garlic very thinly and toss together with the vegetables. Add fresh sage and thyme to taste. Toss with enough olive oil to coat. Roast in a covered pan at 375° for 30 minutes, then uncover and bake 5 to 10 minutes more, or until vegetables are lightly browned and tender. Garnish with additional fresh sage and thyme sprigs.

LEMON-GARLIC
CHRISTMAS OLIVES

One of the beauties of this recipe is that you can prepare the olives early in December and keep them in the refrigerator, ready to go, until Christmas. This recipe will yield a little more than 10 ounces. I usually triple it, fill small jars to give away and keep one large jar for us.

Drain the olives and reserve the brine. Rinse the olives and drain very well. Place them in the bottom of a clean, sterilized jar. Then add, in layers, oregano, garlic, lemon and peppercorns. Add the lemon juice and enough of the reserved brine to fill to the top. Cover the jar with a tight-fitting lid, then shake gently. Let the olives marinate at least a week in the refrigerator before serving.

Makes about 10 ounces.

1	10-ounce jar large green Spanish olives with pimiento
3–5	fresh oregano sprigs or 1 teaspoon dried
3	large garlic cloves, peeled and crushed
2–4	lemon wedges
10	whole black or green peppercorns
3–4	tablespoons fresh lemon juice

Simple and delicious—Roast Loin of Pork with Prunes and Apples (page 81), Root Vegetables Roasted with Sage and Thyme.

CHEDDAR CROQUETTES WITH TOMATO CHUTNEY

Served on colorful kale leaves, croquettes make a splendid hors d'oeuvre. And the combination of the hot, cheesy croquettes and the sweet, sharp, fresh chutney is addictive. You can cook the croquettes ahead of time and reheat them in the oven just before serving.

To make the chutney: Place the sugar, raisins, salt, pepper, mustard seed, allspice and vinegar in a large nonaluminum saucepan and bring to a boil. Add the tomatoes and shallots and simmer slowly, uncovered, until the mixture is thick, at least 45 minutes. Put in clean, sterilized pint or half-pint mason jars and cover tightly. (You can also put the chutney in decorative pots, but make sure you seal them tightly.) This will keep, like jam, for several months in your refrigerator.

To make the croquettes: Melt the butter in a medium saucepan, whisk in the flour and cook over low heat for 10 minutes. In a separate pan, bring the milk to a boil and gradually whisk it into the flour and butter. Whisk constantly, cooking until the sauce is very thick. Remove from heat. Stir in the yolks one at a time, then the cheese and chives or scallions. Beat until everything is well combined. Refrigerate 6 to 8 hours, or overnight.

Shape into 18 small balls. Put the flour, with salt and pepper to taste, in a plastic bag, then add the balls and gently shake to coat them. Dip each ball in the beaten egg, then roll it in the bread crumbs until it's thoroughly coated.

Pour canola oil in a large skillet to cover to a depth of 1 inch. Heat the oil to 350°. Fry the balls until they are golden brown, about 4 to 5 minutes. Drain on paper towels or brown paper bags.

Serve the croquettes on a large leaf of red or green kale with a generous scoop of chutney on the side.

Makes 18 croquettes and 7 to 8 cups of chutney.

Tomato Chutney

2	cups sugar
³⁄₄	cup golden raisins
1	tablespoon salt
1	teaspoon freshly ground pepper
3	tablespoons mustard seed
½	teaspoon allspice
3³⁄₄	cups vinegar
3	pounds ripe or 2 large cans (28-ounce size) tomatoes, peeled, seeded and chopped
½	pound shallots, peeled and chopped

Croquettes

½	cup butter
½	cup flour
2	cups milk
2	egg yolks
8	ounces sharp Vermont cheddar cheese, grated
2	tablespoons chives or 2 tablespoons green scallion tops, chopped
½	cup flour (or enough to coat balls)
	Salt
	Pepper
1	egg, beaten
1	cup dried bread crumbs
	Canola oil
4–6	leaves red or green kale or other decorative green (optional)

Sweet and tangy chutney combines with sharp Vermont cheddar cheese to make a delicious appetizer for your meal.

R O A S T   L O I N   O F   P O R K
W I T H   P R U N E S   A N D   A P P L E S

What a handsome platter this is when you thinly slice the delicate tenderloin to show off the mosaic of prunes and apples inside—and the slices glisten with cider sauce.

To make the bread crumbs: Grind the bread into fine crumbs in a food processor. In a medium saucepan, sauté the garlic and herbs for about 3 minutes in the butter, long enough to just release their flavor. Mix with the bread crumbs.

To make the roast: Place the rib bones in a large roasting pan with the onions, carrots and thyme and bake for 20 to 30 minutes at 400°, stirring once. Make a tunnel lengthwise through the middle of the roast with a long, thin knife or a clean sharpening steel. Core the apples, peel them if you like and cut the fruit into 1-inch pieces.

Fill the cavity in the pork loin with alternating prunes and apples, packed in fairly tightly. Season the pork all over with salt and pepper, and roll the roast in the garlic-herb bread crumbs to coat the sides. Place the roast on top of the bones and vegetables in the roasting pan, and bake at 375° for 1 to 1½ hours, or until a meat thermometer reads 160° when inserted into the meaty part of the roast. Remove the roast and vegetables to a warm platter.

To make the cider sauce: While the pork is cooking, boil the cider rapidly in a large nonaluminum pot for at least 15 minutes to reduce it to 1 cup. It should be syrupy. In a separate saucepan, bring the water and sugar to a boil and cook, watching carefully, until it is caramelized (about 10 minutes). Add the vinegar, cook briefly to warm through and add this mixture to the cider, stirring well. When the pork is done, deglaze the roasting pan by pouring the stock into the pan and scraping up the bits with a wooden spoon. Strain and degrease the liquid, and add it to the cider mixture.

To serve: Let the meat rest 15 minutes, then slice the roast thinly, no more than ¼ inch thick. Serve with the warm cider sauce.

Makes 6 generous servings.

Garlic-Herb Bread Crumbs

- ½ loaf fresh French bread, broken into chunks
- 2–3 cloves garlic, finely minced
- 1 teaspoon chopped fresh rosemary or ½ teaspoon dried
- 1 teaspoon chopped fresh thyme or ½ teaspoon dried
- 1 teaspoon chopped fresh parsley or ½ teaspoon dried
- 2–3 tablespoons butter, melted

Pork

- 3–4 pounds boneless pork loin
- Rib bones from the roast
- 2 large onions, peeled and coarsely chopped
- 2 large carrots, peeled and coarsely chopped
- A few sprigs of fresh thyme or ½ teaspoon dried
- 3 tart apples, such as Northern Spy
- 10 or more pitted prunes
- Salt
- Freshly ground pepper

Cider Sauce

- ½ gallon fresh cider
- ½ cup water
- ½ cup sugar
- ¼ cup cider vinegar
- 1 cup chicken stock

RED POTATOES BAKED IN PARCHMENT

Allow two small to medium potatoes per person. Scrub the potatoes and cut them in half. Toss them with ½ cup of olive oil and 1 teaspoon of chopped fresh rosemary (or ½ teaspoon dried). Lay out one rectangle of parchment paper per serving. Place the potatoes in the center of the paper. Add a sprig of rosemary and a flattened garlic clove on top. Fold the edges of the long sides of the parchment together tightly and twist the ends closed. Bake at 375° for 35 to 45 minutes.

HOLIDAY BUFFET

MARY'S ROAST TURKEY WITH APPLE-SAGE DRESSING
ROAST LEG OF VENISON WITH RED WINE SAUCE
WILD RICE WITH DRIED FRUITS AND NUTS
MARION'S CHILLY DILLY CARROTS
TINY ROLLS SERVED IN A BREAD BASKET (PAGE 51)
WOODSTOCK INN EGGNOG
KEDRON VALLEY INN DOUBLE CHOCOLATE TRUFFLE CAKE

HOLIDAY BUFFET

We almost always have a holiday party for our neighbors, our friends, our children's friends and, of course, whatever relatives are nearby. It's an all-ages party, a great opportunity for stuffing small children into those beautiful little velvet dresses and suits that their grandparents invariably give them. If you have enough young people with a wide-enough age spread, I find they will all amuse each other and give their parents some badly needed time to enjoy themselves unencumbered.

In addition to the adult buffet, I like to have a slightly lower children's table with what we used to call "nursery food" (tuna fish, chicken or egg salad sandwiches, grapes, celery and carrot sticks). But don't be surprised when the toddlers stand on tiptoe to reach the wild rice while the adults (including this one) reach down to scoop up one tiny crustless sandwich after another.

The eye-catching appeal of the turkey and the bread basket belie the actual simplicity of this buffet, which offers a variety of textures and tastes, yet allows the host and hostess to forget about cooking and just enjoy their guests. Everything on the menu below can be made ahead of time and, except for the rolls, served at room temperature. I heat up the rolls and the bread basket (see the recipe on page 51) in the oven and keep them on a warming tray. Once the food is on the sideboard, I'm just another one of the guests.

A self-basting turkey comes out crisp and juicy every time.

MARY'S ROAST TURKEY

My friend Mary O'Connor used to have a turkey farm in Billerica, Massachusetts. Thanks to Mary, I now know how to roast a fat turkey without getting up before dawn and spending the day basting it.

The traditional country dressing I've included is from the Woodstock Inn in Woodstock, Vermont. It is enlivened by the addition of chopped nuts and brandy-soaked currants.

To make the dressing: In a medium skillet, melt the butter and sauté the onion, celery and apples in it for about 5 minutes, or until the onions are translucent. Remove from heat and mix in the bread cubes and seasonings. Add enough milk or stock to just moisten the mixture, then add the eggs and thoroughly combine. Add the nuts and currants, if desired.

To make the turkey: Choose a fresh bird with a nice, plump breast. Allow about ¾ pound per person. This recipe is for a 10- to 12-pound turkey. Rinse the cavity and pat the bird dry. Do not salt the cavity. Stuff *loosely* with dressing. Sew, truss or skewer shut the opening.

Knead the butter together with pepper and herbs to prepare self-basting butter rolls. Divide this mixture in half. Roll each half into a thin sausage about as long as the breastbone. Make pockets under the skin on either side of the breastbone with your finger or a wooden spoon handle. Carefully slip each butter roll under the skin.

Massage the outside skin of the bird with a little butter or the butter wrapper, lightly buttering the breast, legs, thighs and wings. Tuck the wing tips under and tie the legs together. Place the bird on a rack in a roasting pan breast side up and put it, uncovered, into a 450° oven. Turn the oven down to 350° and roast for 2½ hours.

Baste the bird regularly after the first hour of cooking. By then, the "self-basting" butter under the skin will have melted, and the bird will begin to render its own fat. The bird is done when a meat thermometer inserted in the thigh registers 180° and the thigh, when pricked, releases a clear juice. Remove it from the oven and transfer it to a platter. Let the turkey rest for at least 20 minutes before carving.

Makes a generous 5 cups of stuffing and enough turkey to serve 10 to 15 hungry people.

ROAST CAPON OR GOOSE

If you aren't feeding the multitudes, you might want to choose a tender, plump capon or goose instead of a turkey. Follow the same directions, roasting at 350° for 18 to 20 minutes per pound. Allow ¾ pound of capon per person, or 1 to 1½ pounds per person for goose. The Apple-Sage Dressing is a perfect complement, no matter which bird makes your holiday dinner.

Apple-Sage Dressing

¼	cup butter
¼	cup chopped onion
1	cup chopped celery
2	tart apples, peeled, cored and chopped
4	cups cubed, crustless day-old white or wheat bread or corn-bread
¼	cup chopped fresh parsley
1	teaspoon dried sage
1	teaspoon salt
½	teaspoon paprika
⅛	teaspoon freshly grated nutmeg
	Milk or chicken stock
3	eggs
1½	cups chopped nuts (optional): Brazil, pine, pecans, walnuts, filberts or native New England butternuts
¾	cup currants soaked in brandy (optional)

Turkey

10–12	pound turkey
5–6	cups dressing
1	stick (¼ pound) butter
	Freshly ground pepper
	Sage, rosemary, thyme or tarragon (optional)

ROAST LEG OF VENISON WITH RED WINE SAUCE

Pheasant, quail, partridge, duck, rabbit and venison, having long been traditional fare for hunters, are suddenly being touted as the food of the future. But it is not as contradictory as one might think—this low-fat game is farm-raised and completely free of chemicals, hormones and additives.

The venison I use comes from Old Moses Farm in South Strafford, Vermont. I've discovered that when you order venison, you may as well order the bones and trimmings, too, and make up the game stock. It will keep about a year in the freezer. A little of this rich stock will enhance almost any soup or sauce.

To make the stock: Place the bones, trimmings and oil in a large roasting pan and roast uncovered at 450° for 30 minutes. Peel and chop the onion, carrot and parsnip. Lower the oven temperature to 400° and add the vegetables and garlic to the bones. Roast for another 20 minutes.

Remove the pan from the oven and with a slotted spoon, transfer the bones and vegetables to a large saucepan. Add enough of the water to cover the bottom of the roasting pan by about an inch and return to the oven for 10 more minutes to soften the scrapings. Remove from the oven and scrape all the solid bits from the bottom of the pan. Pour this liquid over the browned bones in the saucepan.

Add the remaining water to the bones and slowly bring to a boil. When the stock is just about to boil, turn down the heat and simmer, skimming the foam from the top. Add the herbs, peppercorns and salt. Continue to simmer for 2 to 3 hours, skimming occasionally. Remove the bones and vegetables with a slotted spoon and strain the stock through several thicknesses of cheesecloth. Cool and refrigerate. Remove any solidified fat from the top before using or freezing.

To make the roast: Preheat the oven to 400°. Rub the venison with salt, pepper and butter. Roast the venison in a large roasting pan with the oil for 30 minutes. Lower the temperature to 375° and roast for another 30 minutes, basting occasionally. Stir in all the vegetables, herbs and tomato paste and roast for another 20 minutes. Remove the venison and wrap it in foil to keep it warm.

Add the flour to the pan juices and cook it on the stove for 2 to 3 minutes. Deglaze the pan with the brandy and wine. Boil rapidly to reduce the liquid by half. Add the game stock and simmer for 25 minutes. Strain the sauce, pressing the cooked vegetables through a sieve. Stir in the cranberry jelly and add salt and pepper if desired. Remove the foil from the venison, return the meat to the pan, pour the sauce over and return to the oven for 10 minutes. Place the roast on a heated platter and carve the meat against the grain. Serve the sauce in a heated gravy boat or pitcher.

Makes 10 cups of stock; roast serves 10.

Game Stock

3	pounds game bones and meat trimmings, chopped
1/4	cup canola or olive oil
1	medium onion
1	carrot
1	parsnip
2	cloves garlic, flattened and peeled
14	cups cold water
1/2	teaspoon dried thyme
3	bay leaves
10	juniper berries
20	peppercorns
1	tablespoon salt

Roast Leg of Venison

1	5-pound hind leg of venison, trimmed
	Salt and freshly ground pepper to taste
2	tablespoons butter
3	tablespoons olive or canola oil
1	medium onion, peeled and chopped
1	carrot, chopped
2	bay leaves
25	black peppercorns
1	teaspoon dried thyme
10	juniper berries, crushed
1	tablespoon tomato paste
4	tablespoons flour
1/4	cup brandy
1	cup dry red wine
2	cups game stock
4	tablespoons cranberry jelly

WILD RICE
WITH DRIED FRUITS AND NUTS

For years, I thought this was my very own invention, but in the past couple of years, I have seen several first cousins in new cookbooks. This is one of those recipes that can change, depending on what ingredients you have on hand. Roast chestnuts would be a stellar addition, though it does take extra time to peel them.

In a large mixing bowl, combine the rice, vegetables, fruits and orange zest. Mix gently with a large spatula. Put the juices, salt, pepper, mustard and olive oil in a small jar with a tightly fitting lid and shake vigorously. (This mixture can be made ahead and refrigerated for a day or so.) Add the dressing to the rice, mixing well to blend. Just before serving, sprinkle the parsley and the nuts into the rice, and lightly toss to combine. Serve in a wreath of fresh watercress and thin, decorative orange slices.

Makes 12 servings.

2	cups cooked wild rice
1	cup cooked brown or white rice
½	cup finely chopped celery
½	cup finely chopped scallions (white and green parts)
¼	cup finely chopped red onion
½	cup golden raisins
½	cup chopped dried apricots, plumped in brandy (applejack is the best)
¾	cup dried cherries or cranberries, plumped in brandy (any type will do)
3	tablespoons finely shredded orange zest (no pith)
3	tablespoons fresh orange juice
1	tablespoon fresh lemon juice
1	teaspoon salt
1	teaspoon freshly ground pepper
½	teaspoon Dijon mustard
½	cup olive oil
½	cup chopped Italian parsley
1	cup pecans, hazelnuts or chestnuts, toasted and barely chopped
	Watercress (optional)
	Orange slices (optional)

CHILDREN'S BUFFET

Christmas is a time for families, and especially children. Although there are some children who are content with exotic adult fare, here are some suggestions for the more typical young guests.

On a lowish table, have a platter or two of tiny, crustless sandwiches cut out with Christmas cookie cutters. I use thinly sliced white bread (the children's parents are scandalized) and fillings of tuna fish, egg salad or sometimes chicken.

I make sure to put in a lot of mayonnaise and no celery, lettuce or other green things. And I spread the filling sparingly so that it doesn't ooze out the sides—nothing turns children off more than oozing sandwiches.

If you are feeling especially festive, you can serve the sandwiches on a big, flat basket made out of bread, like the one shown on page 51.

Garnish the sandwich plates with tiny clusters of red and green seedless grapes. Scatter a few little plates of raw carrot and celery sticks around. Make a simple children's punch with ginger ale, a tiny bit of Grenadine syrup (not enough to stain their clothes or your upholstery) and orange slices and serve it with lots of ice.

For dessert, fill up the Gingerbread Sleigh on page 12 with Christmas cookies and tiny candy canes, but leave it out of sight until most of the sandwiches have disappeared.

MARION'S CHILLY DILLY CARROTS

My sister-in-law Marion made these refreshing carrots for me once long ago. They are pungent with dill and revolutionized my attitude toward this underused herb. Don't be shocked by the ginger ale—it has a mysterious way of not just sweetening and counteracting the vinegar, but making the carrots more carroty tasting.

Bring the ginger ale to a boil in a large skillet and add the carrots. Turn down the heat and gently cook the carrots, covered, until they are just tender. Drain. In a large bowl, mix together the onion, dill, vinegar, oils, salt and sugar. Add the carrots while they are still warm. Cover the bowl loosely and refrigerate until ready to serve.

Makes 12 servings.

1½	cups ginger ale
3½	pounds carrots, cut into 2-inch matchsticks
1	large sweet Spanish onion, peeled and finely chopped
½–1	cup chopped fresh dill, depending on your taste
¼	cup white wine vinegar
¼	cup canola oil or peanut oil
2	tablespoons olive oil
½–1	teaspoon salt, depending on your taste
½	teaspoon sugar

The Christmas classic—served up with colorful Christmas Tree Wafers (page 9).

WOODSTOCK INN EGGNOG

This is the classic eggnog recipe. But we've modified it so the eggs are cooked rather than raw to avoid any danger of salmonella contamination.

In a large saucepan, beat the egg yolks with 1 cup of the sugar and the salt until very light. In a separate bowl, beat the egg whites until they are stiff. Slowly beat the remaining ½ cup of sugar into the whites. Thoroughly fold the whites into the yolks.

Whip the cream until it's stiff enough to hold its shape. Thoroughly beat the cream into the saucepan, then add the milk. Cook the mixture over low heat, stirring constantly, until the mixture thickens and just coats a metal spoon. Remove from heat.

Stir in the brandy and beat well. Beat in rum. Chill briefly. Grate fresh nutmeg over the top just before serving.

Makes about 1 gallon.

12	eggs, separated
1½	cups sugar
¼	teaspoon salt
1	quart heavy cream
1	quart milk
1	quart brandy (or half brandy, half bourbon)
1	cup rum
	Freshly grated nutmeg to taste

Kedron Valley Inn Double Chocolate Truffle Cake (page 90) is sure to delight the most devoted chocolate-lover.

KEDRON VALLEY INN DOUBLE CHOCOLATE TRUFFLE CAKE

The unbelievably rich layers of this cake are composed of two kinds of mousse. You can make the two mousses a few days ahead—along with the sponge cake—then freeze all the parts until you are ready to assemble them. The glaze, however, needs to be prepared just before serving.

None of the steps is difficult, but if you try to do them all at once it might seem like an endless project. If you could eat a piece first, before you roll up your sleeves, you will never question why you are doing this. This cake is the crowning glory of any holiday party.

To make the sponge cake: In a small saucepan over low heat, melt the chocolate in the milk. Remove from heat and let cool.

Sift the cake flour, then sift a second time with the baking powder and salt. In a large mixing bowl, beat the egg yolks with the confectioners' sugar and vanilla until lemon-colored. Add the cooled chocolate mixture, then fold in the flour mixture.

In a separate bowl, beat the egg whites at high speed with an electric mixer until they hold stiff peaks. Fold into the chocolate mixture. Pour into an ungreased 10-inch springform pan. Bake at 350° for 50 minutes or until a toothpick inserted into the center of the cake comes out clean. Cool thoroughly, then remove from the pan.

To make the white chocolate mousse: Mix 3 ounces of the cream with the butter and sugar in a small heavy saucepan and bring to a full boil. Put the chocolate in the work bowl of a food processor and, with the motor running, pour the hot mixture in through the feed tube. Continue to process until the chocolate has melted. Add the egg yolk and pulse until combined. Transfer this mixture to a bowl and cool to 86° to 90°.

If you don't have a food processor, grate the chocolate and add it to the saucepan (off the heat), stirring until the chocolate is melted. If necessary, warm the mixture over low heat to finish the melting process. Beat in the egg yolk and transfer the mixture to a bowl and cool to 86° to 90°.

Whip remaining cream until stiff, and fold it into the chocolate mixture. Refrigerate until ready to use (no more than a day or so).

To make the dark chocolate mousse: Mix 3 ounces of the cream with the sugar in a small heavy saucepan and bring to a full boil. Combine with the chocolate in a food processor according to the white chocolate mousse recipe. Pulse in rum and egg yolks. (Do this with an electric mixer if you are not using a food processor.) Continue according to directions for white chocolate mousse and refrigerate until ready to use.

To make the buttercream icing: Combine all the ingredients in a small mixing bowl. Beat with an electric mixer on medium speed until light and fluffy.

General Ingredients and Supplies

Chocolate sponge cake

White chocolate mousse

Dark chocolate mousse

1/3 cup apricot jam

1 1/2 cups chocolate buttercream icing

1 cup semi-sweet chocolate, chopped into crumbs

Chocolate glaze

10" × 2" springform cake pan

Chocolate Sponge Cake

4 ounces unsweetened chocolate

1 cup whole milk

1 1/4 cups cake flour

2 1/2 teaspoons baking powder

1/2 teaspoon salt

4 eggs, separated

2 cups confectioners' sugar

1 teaspoon vanilla

White Chocolate Mousse

11 ounces heavy cream

1 teaspoon unsalted butter

1 tablespoon sugar

5 ounces white chocolate, chopped

1 egg yolk

To assemble the cake: Line a 10-inch springform pan with plastic wrap, leaving just enough wrap around the edges to hang over the sides of the pan. Slice the sponge cake carefully into 3 thin, round layers. An easy way to do this is to wrap dental floss or thread around the circumference of the cake, then carefully draw it through, splitting a thin layer off the cake. Place the bottom layer in the pan and spread it with white chocolate mousse. Place the second layer on top of the white mousse and spread it with the dark chocolate mousse. Then place the remaining layer on top.

Refrigerate the cake for 2 or more hours. (It may also be frozen at this stage. But if it has been frozen, you should let the cake thaw in the refrigerator at least 2 hours before serving.) Invert the cake onto a large plate or platter. (What was the top of the cake goes on the bottom.) Spread the new top with apricot jam. Ice the sides with buttercream icing and cover them with the chocolate crumbs. Pipe a border of icing around the top edge. Pour the chocolate glaze into the center and spread it to the edges.

Keep the cake in a cool place until ready to serve.

To make the chocolate glaze: In a small, heavy saucepan, melt the chocolate and water together. When they are melted and combined, test to make sure the glaze is smooth and thoroughly blended: draw a spoon through the mixture, then count to 10 slowly. If the trail of the spoon disappears, the glaze is ready. If not, add a little more water and blend to reach this consistency. Reminder: Make the glaze only when you are ready to serve the cake.

Variations: For a more intense cake, thin the melted chocolate chips for the glaze with very strong coffee instead of water and use seedless black raspberry jam in place of the apricot. To make a vanilla icing instead of chocolate, substitute 1 teaspoon of vanilla for the cocoa.

To make a cake that will serve 12 to 16 people, cut the recipe in half and use a 7-inch springform pan.

Makes 24 to 32 servings.

Dark Chocolate Mousse

11	ounces heavy cream
2	tablespoons sugar
4	ounces bittersweet chocolate, chopped
1	tablespoon dark rum
2	egg yolks

Buttercream Icing

1/3	cup unsalted butter, softened
3	cups confectioners' sugar
3–4	tablespoons heavy cream
1/2	cup unsweetened dark cocoa

Chocolate Glaze

1/2	cup chocolate chips
1/4	cup water

A rustic barn is the perfect setting for a tree-trimming party.

CHAPTER SEVEN

VERMONT CELEBRATIONS

echoes of yesteryear

From the quiet town of Shelburne, nestled along the eastern shore of Lake Champlain, right on south to Woodstock and Perkinsville—throughout all of Vermont—the Christmases of New England's past continue to echo in the folding hills and river valleys. Soaring church spires, sturdy covered bridges and white clapboard houses have all graced this beautiful landscape for more than a century with a simple, steadfast dignity. We are wrapped in timelessness here, where the enduring past seems to securely anchor us in the present, and even give promise to our tomorrows.

I find such a flood of history especially interesting in this, the newest of all the New England states. Vermont was settled relatively late, and began as part of New York and part of New Hampshire. Not until 1791 did Vermont join the Union as the fourteenth state, and the churches and farms that make us think of olden times were probably built in the nineteenth century—relative newcomers compared to Plimoth Plantation or Deerfield Village in Massachusetts. But Vermonters cherish their heritage, respect it and keep it alive, particularly at Christmas.

Throughout Vermont, the Christmas festivities begin early in December. My travels take me from historic Shelburne, on the shores of Lake Champlain, south to Woodstock, just in time for the Wassail Weekend activities. While in the Woodstock area, I stop to take in Billings Farm and Museum, a nineteenth-century agricultural farm, and the wonders of Quechee Gorge.

My final stop this holiday season is in Perkinsville on Christmas Day, when I join the celebration at the Inn at Weathersfield, an eighteenth-century hostelry nestled on 12 acres at the foot of Hawks Mountain.

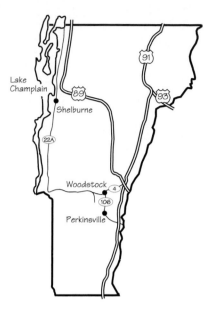

Stockings are hung by the chimney with care in the Stone Cottage at the Shelburne Museum.

The expansive grounds of the Shelburne Museum.

SHELBURNE—THE RICH AND THE POOR

It's a still, cold night early in December when I visit the expansive 45-acre grounds of the Shelburne Museum. This settlement is far more than an ordinary museum. Founded by Electra Havemeyer Webb, the daughter of well-known collectors of European and Asian art and herself an avid collector, it is an eclectic preservation of diverse New England culture. The offerings here include a Lake Champlain lighthouse, now perched on the hillside, and an old side-wheeler—a steamboat with a paddle wheel on each side—hard aground on the slope just below. But I pay little attention to these two relics, barely visible in the gathering dusk.

Instead, I focus on the beckoning cluster of houses ahead of me, where soft lamplight spills from small-paned windows into the deepening December dark. Carols rise from the Meeting House, and children's voices call across the winter-tidy gardens and narrow walkways where we stroll among the softly glowing lights. No cars are allowed in here. Except for the rustle of ripstop nylon jackets, I'd hardly believe I was still in the twentieth century. Visitors to the Shelburne Museum glimpse a moment of the nineteenth century, frozen in time. I hear the rhythmic jangle of harness bells and a patient whinny, and turn to see an old coach drawn by huge Belgian draft horses.

Candles and luminaria light the wintry night at Shelburne.

Once inside the ring of houses, my first stop is the Tuckaway General Store to get some idea of how nineteenth-century New Englanders did their Christmas shopping. The old-fashioned pot-bellied stove greets me as I enter this crowded, bright room. Baskets filled with fragrant pine and cedar cones, nuts, oranges or polished apples stand on the counters and the floor. Woolen socks and mittens hang in pairs from a little clothesline, and giant red long johns droop with emptiness.

Beside the tall biscuit barrel stands a sparse little pine tree, garlanded with cranberries and popcorn. Bolts of calico and ribbons galore seem more festive here than any lavish department store display I've seen so far. I am struck by the simple things once offered for sale—needles, thread, scissors, a new knife—and how great their worth. An orange would have been, I think, a glorious gift to a Vermont child a hundred years ago.

I leave the warmth of the store and discover how very cold it is outside. Lights lure me to the Prentis House, the house of an early nineteenth-century prosperous New England doctor. As I enter, I see company is expected; the tea service is laid out in the dining room, and little cakes and sweetmeats wait in the parlor, along with pipes, snuff and tobacco. The decorations are appealingly simple—a heavy pewter bowl filled with ruby apples and a few evergreen sprigs, pine and cedar boughs in a satin-finished pewter tankard.

On my way to the Dutton House next door, I stop by the long shed to visit the woolly sheep, goats and chickens, looking peaceful and warm. They stir as I enter, then settle back to their feed.

Inside the Dutton House, an atmosphere of Puritan austerity surrounds me. Home to Samuel Dutton, a prominent member of the community, it displays the conservative attitudes of the times—baskets filled with clothes, food and other necessities wait by the door, all ready to be delivered to the poor. On the dining room table stands a pyramid made of apples, and in the living room, a spindly pine tree decorated with a few paper ornaments and gilded nuts.

A bare-branched Christmas tree at the Shelburne Museum.

Dinner is underway in the big kitchen, with a goose poised on an ingenious spit in a reflector oven. Set on the hearth in front of the fireplace, the spit was turned by a clock jack—a device made from the movement of an old tall clock. The movement was connected to the spit—once wound, the spit turned as regularly as the hands of the clock once did.

On the long harvest table, bowls of nuts, mincemeat and green tomato pickles are set out alongside crocks of citron and a few mince pies. Parker House rolls (the original recipe—not packaged and frozen) are rising in a big bowl, and the onion sauce is on the hearth. Jenny Hermenze of the New England Culinary Institute is happy to share her nineteenth-century recipes for onion sauce and Parker House rolls (opposite page).

From the Dutton House, I cross the lane to the Sea Captain's house. The flavor here is different—exotic with silk and porcelain from the Orient, rich brocade from France and English dolls. In the kitchen, women are busy making pomander balls with oranges and cloves and turning grapes into sugar plums with an icy coating of sugar and egg whites.

My favorite house is the poorest. The Stone Cottage, a tiny dwelling with a single room on the ground floor and a sleeping loft above, was home to an immigrant Irish family with at least three children. The Christmas tree here is only a bare branch stuck into a mug and decorated with a chain of wooden shaving curls and paper dolls holding hands. A nearly finished child's dress—a Christmas present, I am sure—waits patiently beside the sewing basket for the last stitches.

Over the fireplace hang the children's stockings. I wonder if one of them will hold an orange on Christmas morning. Bread is rising in a pot on the hearth. But in the middle of the small room is a truly grand present—a wooden sled. It looks like a king's ransom in this humble room.

PAST TIMES' PASTIMES

Next, I visit the Meeting House, perfectly proportioned and decorated by two unadorned trees. Inside, it is full of people, carols and the scent of spruce. Outside it is beginning to snow, lazy flakes right now, but the air is cold and I feel the wind picking up a bit. On the lawn in front of the Dutton House, I stop for a moment by the huge bonfire to warm my hands before continuing on to the Schoolhouse.

Like the general store, the heart of the Schoolhouse is the stove. Minute by minute, I am developing a new and mighty respect for heat. Christmas cards lie on each scarred desk, in varying states of completion. They are made of assorted materials—bits of lace, ribbon, colored and shiny paper, fluffy pieces of cotton and wool, probably carefully saved throughout the year for just this purpose. These are real creations, almost more like valentines.

An old-fashioned flour bin at the Shelburne Museum.

FROM THE KITCHENS OF THE SHELBURNE MUSEUM

Jenny Hermenze of the New England Culinary Institute pitched in to help the Shelburne Museum celebrate a real old-fashioned Christmas. She swears by these authentic recipes from The Homestead, *a Vermont magazine published in the 1870s. Although exact quantities aren't given, Jenny says you can't go wrong.*

ONION SAUCE

Boil a dozen onions until tender, then chop them fine. Make a sauce of milk, well-thickened with flour. Add a little butter and salt. Boil the sauce, then add the chopped onions. Send to the table hot.

PARKER HOUSE ROLLS

Combine 1 quart (4 cups) of flour, 2 tablespoonfuls of sugar, 2 tablespoonfuls of butter (rubbed into the flour), ½ cup of yeast (see recipe below, or use 2 packages active dry yeast) and 1 pint (2 cups) of warm milk. (If you use the active dry yeast, be sure to dissolve it completely in the warm milk before mixing all the ingredients together.) Stir this up at night and put it into a large bowl to rise overnight. In the morning, stir in enough flour to have it knead without sticking, then put it back in the same bowl to rise again. When it is risen nice and light (doubled in bulk), form it into rolls. Keep the dough warm until teatime (or at least 20 minutes), then bake in a quick (425°) oven until brown.

Makes about 2 dozen rolls.

PARKER HOUSE YEAST

On Monday, boil 1 ounce of your best hops in 2 quarts of water for 15 minutes. Strain and cool slightly. Add a small handful of salt and ¼ pound of sugar. Beat ½ pound of flour with a little of this mixture until smooth, then add the remaining mixture and blend well. Let stand in a warm place, stirring occasionally. On Wednesday, add 1½ pounds boiled, mashed potatoes. Let stand until Thursday, then bottle for later use.

The school Christmas tree is decorated with dozens of little American flags, paper stars and swans, milkweed pods and pinecones. And of course, the ubiquitous cranberry and popcorn chains. Candles in candlesticks made from apples line the window sills. I must remember to try that at home.

Now I press on to the Webb Gallery for a glimpse of the tabletop Victorian tree, decorated with a handful of old hand-blown silvered glass ornaments, tinsel garlands, lithographed paper ornaments and real candles. The silver has yellowed a bit over the years and the whole effect of the tree is fragile and rare. It reminds me of my great-grandmother's silk wedding dress, shredding with age, with seed pearls and fabric the color of weak tea. I inspect one last precious ball held in a web of golden thread so fine it might have been spun by a spider.

Outside, the snow is really coming down and I skid my way to what is called the Variety Unit. Here, in the Pewter Room, a greens demonstration is taking place. We learn how to make evergreen ropes and swags, then move on to decorative fruit pyramids. The bases for the pyramids are deceptively simple—wooden cones studded with nails to impale the fruit and to twine the background greenery around.

In the Teapot Room next door, the air is quiet and charged with competition. Seated at a number of small tables are people of all ages, deeply involved in a variety of board games—Parcheesi, checkers, backgammon, chess—and I am reminded that before the days of television, Christmas celebrations were active. Families played together, danced, sang songs, put on plays.

Upstairs, I am pleased to find the dolls all ready for Christmas in their best dresses, some with velvet coats, fur muffs and fancy bonnets. Tiny trees and presents wait in doll house parlors, and plaster turkeys cool on miniature platters. Several artisans who recreate some of the museum dolls and toys are demonstrating just how they do it—one pours bisque base into molds, another shows how to perfect a doll's hairdo. It's a little like Santa's workshop up here, and I like it.

Next, I hurry to the Hat and Fragrance Unit, where children are busy making old-time crafts. Some are working on small hand-carved and painted animals based on those in the museum's Circus Parade; others print Christmas cards on century-old presses. There must be 40 or so children at work here, from toddlers to teens, and I think with pleasure of the many dark television sets in Shelburne tonight.

Back outside, I follow the twinkling lights, pausing for a few minutes in the opening of the covered bridge, a real refuge from the snow which has become deliciously heavy. The Shelburne Museum world is very white, cold and quiet now. Almost everyone has left, and only footprints and hoofprints on the snowy walkways attest to the earlier crowd. Just beyond the handsome round barn, the parking lot comes into view, making my heart sink just a

Winter outside the Sawyer's Cabin at the Shelburne Museum.

little as the present returns. I look back once more over my shoulder into the silent past; I have been a time traveler tonight. With a sigh, I get in the car and buckle up, revving into the last decade of the twentieth century.

W OODSTOCK
THEN AND NOW

The next stop in my Vermont Christmas is Woodstock, to celebrate Wassail Weekend. I wonder as I walk through this picture-perfect village the day before the Wassail begins to flow, if this place will be a zoo tomorrow, with droves of tourists (flatlanders, they're called). I decide to explore Woodstock now, in relative quiet.

The village boundaries are outlined by the Ottauquechee River to the east and Kedron Brook to the west, both of which wind between Mount Tom and Mount Peg; Hartland Hill is to the south. The deep winter freeze hasn't locked in yet, and the water runs black between the white-layered tongues of ice that extend from the banks. There is a little dusting of snow on the ground—enough to turn the fields white but not enough to cover the tawny corn-stubble and not enough for a sleigh ride.

Too bad, because I'd hoped to get Paul Kendall, owner of the 45-horse Kedron Valley Stable (as well as a fleet of historic sleighs and carriages) to take me skimming across the countryside. Paul, a sixth-generation Woodstock native and former owner of the historic Kedron Valley Inn, is well known for his summer and fall inn-to-inn treks on horseback through some of New England's most beautiful woodlands and fields.

Why limit the treks to good weather, I wondered? Couldn't we ride a horse or sleigh or carriage, or ski from inn to inn in the winter? Yes, Paul tells me, we can. All the places to eat and stay mentioned here can be part of a winter holiday where, with Paul's help, you can leave your car and the modern world behind.

Just crossing one of the three covered bridges, and looking down Elm Street festooned with simple greens and American flags, helps me shed some of my twentieth-century impatience and frenzy. Woodstock isn't old-old, like Nantucket, Massachusetts, or Mystic, Connecticut. The first farmer-homesteaders didn't begin to open up the dense woodlands until the 1770s. But by 1787, Woodstock was the shire town of Windsor County. Mills and brickyards had sprouted along the river, and the town bustled with leather workers, silversmiths, tinsmiths and shopkeepers.

But it was the abundance of professional men, particularly lawyers, that made Woodstock prosper. Their graceful homes—more than a century old—circle the green and line Elm and Pleasant streets, reminders of the era when Woodstock became one of the earliest and most prestigious centers of culture in Vermont.

The stagecoach lines that crossed New England used Woodstock as a transfer station, generating a need for liveries and inns. Richardson's Tavern opened in 1783 on the site of the current Woodstock Inn, and travelers have found refreshment on this spot ever since.

By 1875, trains had replaced stage coaches and, with the founding of the Woodstock Railroad Company, Woodstock was one of the first American towns to shift from a rural economy to tourism. I find Woodstock's hundred-plus years of resort experience comforting in the face of the upcoming weekend and, determined not to worry about the influx of flatlanders, I set out for Simon Pearce's restored mill in Quechee. I drive along the unpaved River Road, a narrow 4-mile beauty that hugs the north bank of the Ottauquechee River. Next time I'll walk it instead, admiring the covered bridges as I go.

GLASSBLOWING
AND MAGICAL STARS

For nearly 200 years, a variety of gristmills, sawmills and woolen mills operated where the Simon Pearce facility stands, making it the nucleus of the town of Quechee. But the last woolen mill finally closed in 1967, and the property was turned into offices. In 1980, Irish glassblower Simon Pearce purchased the building along with the dam and the water rights. Pearce moved his glassblowing operation from Kilkenny, Ireland, across the

Making a lamp at the Simon Pearce workshop in Quechee, Vermont.

A water jug and inscribed baby bowl from Simon Pearce.

Atlantic to the dam-level bottom floor of the mill. He replaced the old cement dam with a hydroelectric dam and installed a turbine. The power generated here feeds right into the Central Vermont power grid, and is more than enough to power the Simon Pearce furnaces.

The mill is now once again the focus of Quechee, attracting visitors to its first-class restaurant overlooking the falls, as well as the museum-like showroom of Pearce's glass and pottery and the workshops below. This is where I watch, spellbound, as lithe glass-blowers work in pairs like practiced dancers moving from furnace to furnace, turning globs of molten glass into icy beauty. They move quickly, these artisans, while I hold my breath at their fragile magic.

Dark comes early in the mountains, and night is falling fast as I head back to Woodstock. I see a huge star shining above the village and the inky hills. I wonder if I'm dreaming but the star is there all right, leading me on. And like others before me, I follow, dazzled by such a sight. At the foot of Pleasant Street I stop, for right there the star appears directly above the graceful spire of the First Congregational Church, as if placed there on purpose.

I forgo the Wassail Ball for the best mushroom soup ever and a game of darts at the Skunk Hollow Tavern in Hartland Four Corners. Skunk Hollow Road was a major thoroughfare for stage-coaches, and the tavern, with its narrow hand-pressed bricks and sloping sills, continues to be a popular stop. Here I learn that the star I saw earlier is perched atop Mount Tom and has been shining off and on for about 50 years, the handiwork of the local electric company.

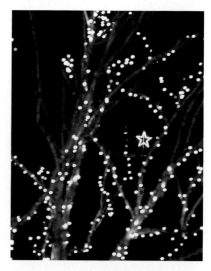

The star on Mount Tom shines brightly through the twinkling lights.

WASSAIL DAY AT LAST

The next morning from my tower-top silo bedroom in the guest wing of Kitty Bacon's Six Willows Farm bed and breakfast on Hartland Hill, I see Mount Ascutney loom bluish in the cloudy dawn. I can tell it's freezing cold out there by the way Kitty's sheep clump together in the pasture below and by the horses' steamy breath. Today is the Wassail Celebration, and there is a lot going on all over town.

I head out first to the Vermont Institute of Natural Science (VINS), a private, nonprofit nature center. Before I go inside to check out their Holiday Nature Crafts program, I climb the hill behind the VINS building to the Raptor Center, which has huge fenced-in habitats for 25 different species of injured and orphaned owls, falcons, eagles and other raptors who cannot be returned to the wild. Being in the presence of these majestic creatures makes me want to stay here and listen to their squawking and calling— if only it weren't so cold.

Inside the airy auditorium, a few dozen children and grown-ups are hard at work around long, well-supplied tables placed beneath the huge windows. We learn to tie macramé snowflakes, weave paper stars, make spinning tops from frozen orange juice lids and fashion wreaths from dried apple slices. No one cares how young or old you are, and everyone is busy, a fine way to spend a Saturday morning in December. Afterward, I take a quick walk along one of their nature trails, one more look at the birds, and then I'm off to Billings Farm, to see how Vermonters celebrated Christmas in the 1890s.

CHICKEN PIE
AND JACK FROST

In the lovingly restored Queen Anne farmhouse at Billings Farm and Museum, Susan McKee, interpretation specialist and farmhouse manager, furiously beats biscuits with her rolling pin on the sturdy kitchen table. This doesn't feel a bit like a museum to me, nor does it smell like one, with fragrant chicken soup simmering on the back of the six-burner wood stove for the staff's lunch. Susan McKee looks as though she's lived in this friendly kitchen all her life, and I can imagine I have, too. Amazing how easily the twentieth century can vanish—especially in a well-appointed household such as this one.

The story behind Billings Farm is as fascinating as the farm itself. One of Woodstock's most important patrons, Frederick Billings, left Vermont to make a fortune in the Gold Rush as a California lawyer. Billings went on to invest in the Northern Pacific Railway and establish Yosemite National Park. He returned to Woodstock in 1871 and established his model dairy farm. Today,

Biscuits fresh from the oven at the Billings Farm and Museum.

Billings Farm and Museum is immaculately conserved to a large extent through the efforts of Mary French Rockefeller (granddaughter of Frederick Billings) and her husband, Laurance.

More than just the agricultural museum it set out to be, Billings Farm is alive with social history. I pry myself away from the browning biscuits and steaming soup and head for the dining room, where holiday paper crackers, a Jack Horner's Pie with presents, and a real Mince Pie and Scripture Cake wait on the carefully laundered (and neatly darned) damask tablecloth.

Though this was *not* Frederick Billings' house, but the house of his farm manager, it seems very grand to me. The centerpiece is a bowl of pinecones—some lightly gilded and others covered with "snow"—dried yarrow, bittersweet, goldenrod and a few oranges. The snow (made from mucilage and Epsom salts and sometimes cotton) glistens with a sprinkling of mica flakes. I make a note to try this at home. I ask Susan what a Vermont family would have eaten for Christmas Dinner a hundred years ago.

"Chicken Pie," she says, not a missing a beat with her rolling pin. "Chicken Pie was the special holiday meal."

The sitting room has a good-sized tree in the bay window, decorated with handmade gifts such as miniature corncobs that are in fact cylindrical pot holders to slip on hot handles; mittens; a felt pen-wiper—actually not all that different from the presents I used to make my parents only 40 or so years ago.

Scripture Cake, Mince Pie and a Jack Horner's Pie await holiday visitors at the Billings Farm and Museum.

Simple items make lovely centerpieces at Billings Farm.

CHICKEN PIE

Susan McKee, the farmhouse manager at Billings Farm and Museum in Woodstock, is pleased to share an old recipe for chicken pie, the special Vermont holiday meal from 100 years ago.

Boil the chicken pieces until tender. Remove the meat from the bones and season to taste with salt and pepper. Cut the 4 tablespoons of butter into chunks and place in a baking dish large enough to hold all the chicken. Thicken the broth slightly with a little of the flour, then pour it over the chicken. Mix the remaining ingredients into a soft biscuit dough, roll it out into a crust and cover the baking dish. With a sharp knife, cut slashes in the crust to let the steam escape. Bake in a quick (425°) oven until the crust is brown. Serve with any remaining broth on the side.

Makes 8 servings.

2	chickens, cut up
	Salt and pepper to taste
4	tablespoons butter
2	cups chicken broth
5	cups flour
3	teaspoons cream of tartar
1½	teaspoons baking soda
⅔	cup butter
2	cups milk

There are also decorations on the tree—paper fans and flowers, cornucopias filled with nuts, paper chains, pomander balls, paper American flags and candles. The mantel sparkles with frosted sprays of wheat and pine, milkweed and sumac, and a few pinecones. I wonder what these wonderful coarse ice crystals really are. I've never seen anything quite like them. The docent—our tour guide—tells me they are made from alum, a popular astringent in the 1890s and readily available from an apothecary. Now, I learn, alum is harder to find, but if you are lucky enough to lay your hands on a pound, you can turn delicate evergreens and wheat, rye or other grasses into Jack Frost's handiwork.

It is very hard to pry myself out of this solid Victorian world, but I must because it's almost time for the Wassail Parade to start—the showpiece of the weekend. Reluctantly, I close the heavy farmhouse door. On my way to the parade route, I pass the Billings Farm orchard where some apples linger on the lacy branches and glow garnet-colored against the white and tawny slope of snow and stubble. How could any artist improve on that, I wonder, and hurry on across the river.

A CHRISTMAS PARADE

There's time for a mug of cocoa, and I weave through the friendly and not too crowded crowd that has begun to cluster along the parade route. I sit at one of four small tables in what is primarily a flower shop, with a coffee bar on one wall. It is wonderfully warm and humid in here, flowers and greenery everywhere, the perfect spot to warm up. The windows are festooned with wreaths, and I peer through to view the festive gathering—a living Christmas card—on the chilly street outside.

ALUM ICE CRYSTALS

To 1 gallon of boiling water add 1 pound of alum crystals, stirring well to combine. Remove the pot from the stove. Tie greens or grasses in small bunches and tie on a spoon to guide the bunches down as you immerse them in the alum and hot water mixture. Let them stand in the water overnight and in the morning crystals will have formed.

A miniature reindeer heads the Wassail Parade in Woodstock.

Outside, I hear that this year's parade has 56 entries and involves nearly 100 horses and riders. It is late in starting and this, I learn from the knowledgeable people all around me, is most unusual. While I wait, I watch the spectators, looking for those busloads of city folks, but find instead families with babies on their backs, toddlers on their shoulders and dogs tugging at leashes, all greeting each other, swapping news. Everyone seems to know almost everyone else and, in fact, they even greet *me* as though perhaps I lived next door. (I wish I did.)

All at once, I notice a buzzing hush, and from way down Central Street where the parade begins, I hear the faint strains of "God Rest Ye Merry, Gentlemen." We all crane our necks around the corner of Elm and Pleasant and look down the empty street, expecting the first elegant carriage to appear, the first set of costumed riders and prancing horses. But what is this? Something small, something slow.

The crowd is very quiet, and then there's sudden applause. Down the street comes a small, plump reindeer carrying an impressive crown of antlers, pulling a small, bright pony cart with a small, merry Santa. This is a real, live miniature reindeer here, and a live miniature Santa, too, the "merry old elf" himself. We can hardly believe our eyes. The brief delay is now explained. Miniature reindeer have short little legs and can't go as fast as the horses behind them. But no one minds in the least that things are a little late. We'd wait for days, weeks, to see this perfect sight.

The reindeer vanguard passes all too quickly. I sigh, and the kind woman beside me is reassuring. "They always circle the green a few times. Don't worry, you'll see him again." Now I can relax and enjoy the rest of this most unusual parade.

Antique carriage after carriage, all shined and festooned, pass by, carrying seasonally costumed drivers and passengers. Then

Riders in the holiday parade—well dressed for the occasion.

come individual riders, sidesaddle and astride, dignified on their gleaming horses. Proud children ride by, competently controlling fat, naughty ponies. One after another they come, some groups singing carols, everyone waving. The last is almost the best, a dapper gentleman in top hat and tailcoat who weaves gracefully back and forth across the street on roller blades, a large shovel in his hands—the Super-Duper-Pooper-Scooper.

I leave my piece of curb and trot to the village green in time to see the beloved little reindeer doggedly lead everyone twice around the green, antlers bobbing up and down with effort. Yes, he wins, my undisputed favorite of the parade—maybe even the weekend!

THE MEMORY TREE AND CHRISTMAS VISIONS

The horses and riders head for home and the rest of us all assemble on the green around the Yule Log pyre, close but not too close to the Memory Tree, a tall evergreen strung with unlit lights. The Yule Log has been burned throughout the ages to symbolize the triumph of light over darkness, the triumph of Christ over Satan. In Woodstock, they use last year's ashes to light this year's fire. When the blaze is roaring, we turn to the memory tree, and the list of all those who are remembered by a light this Christmas is read off. It is a solemn moment.

We pause here to reflect briefly and then, all at once, the tree seems to leap with the light of hundreds of white bulbs. An accordionist breaks into "Oh Come, All Ye Faithful" and all of us join in singing, our faces flushed in the welcome heat of the bonfire. Dark begins to fall, and gradually we move on down Elm Street to the First Congregational Church to hear the Revere Hand Bell Choir Concert. I look up just before I enter the church and there it is— the great star on Mount Tom, shining directly down on us.

Before I turn my back on Woodstock and head over Hartland Hill, I have one final event to attend, something called Christmas Visions. I have no idea of what this is. I have only been told that it is presented by the Woodstock Recreation Department and that children may go free of charge. I enter the Little Theater, an old stone building beside the river.

The first thing I hear is a very loud and enthusiastic rendition of "The First Noel" played a little raggedly on four brass instruments by four fourth and fifth grade boys. The large building teems with little children and animals. Santa (a very big and jolly Santa) is enthroned in a splendid sleigh on the stage with a short queue of tots waiting to climb on his lap.

Santa has a nifty entourage of elves, about a dozen of them, 4 to 5 feet high and nicely decked out in green and red elf suits and hats. They are bright and helpful and good at marshalling the

Yule logs blaze brightly on the village green.

smaller children. There are lots of Christmas trees around, and along one whole side of this gigantic room runs an electric train. It's big enough to ride on, and people are doing just that.

Downstairs, I discover the Secret Santa Tree, big and covered with names of the neighborhood needy. Children are eagerly asking their parents to pick names off the tree: They will then make or purchase gifts and food for their "adopted" family this Christmas. "Last year we brought Christmas to over 500 people," says an eager teenaged helper.

A large part of the room is concealed behind rather shaky room dividers, with signs plastered all over the makeshift walls reading "SECRET HOUSE—GROWN-UPS STAY OUT!" So of course, in I go, ducking to clear the very small door. Inside, children perch on the edges of folding chairs at several long, paper-covered tables.

What are they working on so eagerly? I look more closely. Presents for parents! I watch a five-year-old make a candle for her mother by rolling a sheet of beeswax around a string wick, gluing the edge, and sprinkling the candle with glitter. Her seven-year-old brother slides into a seat at the next table, where he takes up a hammer and nail, and hammers out a design in a juice-can lid—and it becomes a pierced ornament. He and his sister take their presents to the last table, where they make their own wrapping paper, then scuttle out the other door, with the wrapped presents for their parents under their arms. Oh, those children are pleased, and they should be, too.

THE VITALITY
THAT SETTLED VERMONT

I hate to leave on Sunday, and so I stop off to see Lillian Marcotte, just up Hartland Hill from my bed and breakfast. Lillian lives on one of the most beautiful pieces of land in the world, I think, land that her family has owned and worked since the Revolution. The author of a recently published book about her Vermont childhood, she tells stories that I never tire of hearing.

Today, I ask her about Christmases past, and she tells me how exciting it was when the school finally gave them a whole day off. She used to love going to the community tree in Hartland Four Corners for carols and candy and games, or to her grandmother's house just across the street, where all the aunts and uncles and cousins would gather—for chicken pie, of course (that favorite Vermont Christmas dish).

"We didn't have our own tree. Nobody had any decorations, for one thing. It was the Depression and we needed a roof." Lillian gives me her bright blue honest look. "I know I can get through just about anything," she says to me. "That's what you learned if you survived the Depression." I believe every word, sitting there in

Dear Sally,

I am writing a hasty note to tell you of something that I think you would like for your book. When baking a cake and you are short of eggs, mix the cake, then the very last thing before pouring it into the tin, add 1 heaping tablespoonful of nice, soft, fluffy snow. It does work—my ancestors did this. I think it must be because there is air in the snow and by adding it last, it makes a light cake.

I trust all is well with you.

Affectionately,

Lillian H. Marcotte

Lillian's cozy kitchen on top of the world. Lillian's strength and endurance seem mirrored in the mountains that stretch outside her windows. Hers is the kind of vitality that settled this state.

INTO THE 1700s

Early Christmas Morning, my husband, Upton, and I set out for tiny Perkinsville, Vermont, where Mary Louise and Ron Thorburn have invited us to celebrate an eighteenth-century New England Christmas at the Inn at Weathersfield. The idea of an eighteenth-century New England Christmas troubles me, because I know that New England didn't celebrate Christmas then—it was prohibited by law. (Christmas was considered a solemn holiday—hard work and worship were the approved activities for the day.) On the other hand, I long to take part in the festivities, a partridge shoot with muskets, open-hearth cooking, virginal and dulcimer music performed by R. P. Hale and colonial dancing. Well, I'll pretend this is just an eighteenth-century winter holiday party and not specifically a Christmas celebration.

I've been here twice before, and both times I've felt as though I were stepping back in time and going home. An advertisement from 1811 says the Inn at Weathersfield is "... where the magnates of the city love to come for rural rest and repose," and I think this

Checking the buckets during the sugaring.

WEATHERSFIELD WASSAIL

This wassail simmered all day on the crane in the parlor fireplace at the Inn at Weathersfield on Christmas day. The room filled with its deliciously spicy fragrance. I helped myself often, as did the other guests, yet the cast-iron pot was never empty.

1 gallon apple cider	½ teaspoon vanilla
1 can (6 ounces) frozen orange juice concentrate	1 orange, halved
	8 whole cloves
	8 whole allspice
1 can (6 ounces) frozen lemonade concentrate	1 apple, cored and sliced (peel left on)
½ cup brown sugar	½ lemon, sliced (optional)
2 sticks cinnamon	

Combine the cider, juices, sugar, cinnamon and vanilla in a large pot. Heat just to a simmer.

Stud one half of the orange with the cloves and the other half with the allspice. Add the orange halves, apple slices and lemon slices (if desired). Serve hot.

Makes 4 to 5 quarts

still holds true. Mary Louise and Ron greet us as though they have known us forever, and we immediately feel welcome.

The rambling, antique-filled house, unlike most New England inns, sits well back from the road, its graceful columned portico barely visible at the end of the long, maple-lined driveway. The earliest part of the house was built in 1795 and then added on to again and again. The columns, an unusual touch in this part of New England, were contributed by a southern gentleman, homesick for the old plantation.

We go in the side door to the keeping room where Ann and Chris Curran, friends of the Thorburns, members of the Brigade of the American Revolution and veterans of colonial cooking for the past 15 years, are getting a head start on the Christmas dinner. The keeping room is a small, wood-paneled room dominated by the generous fireplace and beehive oven. Bunches of herbs hang from the beams. Scattered on the hearth are assorted wrought-iron cooking implements whose functions I will soon discover.

Ann is seated on the settle, kneading bread in a plain colonial bodice and long skirt. Chris, in a shirt, waistcoat and farmer's pants, is crouched beside the beehive oven. I've never seen one of these ovens in action, and I am surprised by the breadth and depth of it. Next to Chris, on the hearth, the turkey is already roasting on its spit in the reflector oven.

It's early yet, and there's not much for amateurs to do in the way of helping, so Upton goes for a walk through the woods following trails used for skiing, sleighing and Paul Kendall's horse treks. I join a few other guests in the front parlor, where the fire snaps and bread rises in bowls on the hearth. A pot of hot wassail hangs from the fireplace crane and I ladle myself a cup, not thinking to ask what is in it. I drink another, and then another. The recipe—nonalcoholic—is perfect for Christmas Day.

A WHITE NEW ENGLAND CHRISTMAS

There is a quiet intimacy among the five or six people seated around the simply decorated tree. One gentleman is reading what looks like a new Christmas book; the others are chatting and laughing quietly. It seems as if I've intruded on a group of old friends who are celebrating Christmas together, and I am about to steal away when one of the men gets up and with a courtly bow, introduces himself and the others to me.

"Sit down, sit down," they say, and so I do.

When I inquire where these guests at the inn have come from, they name Arizona, California, England and Nevada. The couple beside me say that they haven't missed a Christmas at the Inn for the past four years. Each year, they say, they meet people from all over who come for a taste of a real old-fashioned New England Christmas.

Later in the day, we all pitch in to churn butter, chop vegetables and stalk partridge with our two musket-wielding militiamen. I am stunned by the warmth and friendship that flourishes here. This is a family, but without the friction and fissures that so often spring up in real, blood families. How does it work, I wonder? Certainly, the genuine goodwill that pours from our host and hostess sets the stage, but there is something more to this. For one thing, we are not just onlookers; we are all participants, all helping, off and on, to prepare the feast. It's not mandatory, and no one has appointed tasks. But miraculously, everything does get done, and I think that in the process we all become cousins.

The day is punctuated by sporadic visits from Harold Grout, the resident poet laureate, always rendering an appropriate verse from Shakespeare or Keats. Harold is irresistible and somehow vaguely familiar—I think I've met him before in Dickens or seen him in an Arthur Rackham illustration. He seems to be partly magic, and the way he shines when he speaks makes me sure of it.

In mid afternoon, R. P. Hale arrives with his dulcimer and virginal (a sixteenth-century instrument that resembles a harpsichord). He's accompanied by his wife and six-year-old daughter, Alicia. Soon music spills from the gathering room, and Alicia scampers in and out in her long colonial skirt and shawl, a new Christmas doll clutched in each arm.

The beehive oven generates tremendous heat—it must be 90° or more in the keeping room—and many of us cool off by dashing outside, where the temperature is about 80 degrees colder. On one such trip, I notice that it is snowing, and I rush back in to spread the news. A charming young couple have come all the way to Vermont from England especially to enjoy a white New England Christmas, and out they come, like children, their tongues outstretched to catch the flakes.

A MINUET
IN THE GATHERING ROOM

Replete after a most substantial Colonial tea, I pull myself away from the table to dress for dinner. I have brought an old-fashioned blouse, a long skirt and my great-great-grandmother's silk shawl. Ann and Mary Louise change into fancy party dresses known in Colonial times as mantuas, and although the style is still Colonial, the fabric and trim on these party frocks transform the women from workers into celebrators.

Chris puts on a glorious embroidered waistcoat that looks just like the one in *The Tailor of Gloucester,* with a frock coat, breeches and white stockings. Ann and Mary Louise have a few extra skirts, mobcaps and fancy bodices, and more than half the

Willing hands prepare for sumptuous dining at the Inn at Weathersfield.

women put on Colonial garb. I notice how differently we behave, dressed up like this, a little more formal, a little less boisterous. We shed our awkwardness. When we walk, we glide, smooth as silk, in our long skirts.

The gathering room, like every room here, is festive with greenery, candles, polished silver and velvet ribbons. R. P. Hale, his frock coat spread gracefully over the virginal bench, moves from one bright song to the next. His box virginal is a work of art, embellished with real gold leaf and crimson detail. He made this himself, and says it is a replica of one that Cortez is supposed to have brought to Mexico City.

I caught a glimpse of R. P. (as he is known) when he arrived in his blue jeans and lumberjack shirt, but now I can't for the life of me integrate that first sight with the eighteenth-century musician playing by candlelight, his hair neatly drawn back like George Washington's, his wrists weightless under lacy cuffs as his fingers dance across the keys. From here on, I give up all claims on the twentieth century.

The book-lined dining room glows in the flickering candlelight. Even the chandeliers are lighted by tapers. Everyone looks much better in this soft light; our edges are smoothed, wrinkles erased, eyes eager. We sit down, 30 of us, at small tables, to steaming bowls of fish chowder or pumpkin-maple-apple soup. When we finish, Mary Louise and Ron call us to the Christmas buffet table, where Mary Louise explains each of the 12 Colonial dishes she has prepared, more than half of them cooked in the beehive oven or on the open hearth.

After dinner, R. P. returns to his virginal, and Chris becomes

---

THOMAS JEFFERSON'S GINGER BEEF

Mary Louise Thorburn of the Inn at Weathersfield makes this ginger beef dish for Christmas dinner. It is delicious cooked in a Dutch oven on the hearth or on your stove top. (Keep an eye on it so it doesn't overcook.) I find the blend of beef, ginger and tomato unexpected and very welcome on a winter's night.

In a bowl, combine the onions, garlic, turmeric, ginger and salt. Add the beef strips, stir to mix and let stand about one hour. Melt the butter or margarine in a Dutch oven and sauté the beef mixture until it is lightly browned. Add the tomatoes and parsley. Cover and simmer for 1½ to 2 hours. Add a little water to prevent the beef from drying out if you need to. This is excellent served with rice or noodles.

Makes 4 servings.

2	onions, peeled and chopped fine
1	clove garlic, peeled and minced
1	teaspoon turmeric
4	teaspoons ground ginger
1½	teaspoons salt
1½	pounds top round or flank steak, cut into ½" strips
¼	cup butter or margarine
1	cup stewed tomatoes
½	cup chopped fresh parsley (or ¼ cup dried)

NOTTINGHAM PUDDING

This pudding, made by Mary Louise Thorburn at the Inn at Weathersfield, is as light as an angel, and more of a soufflé than a pudding. An irresistible delicacy from her Christmas dinner, it was also traditionally cooked on the open hearth.

Cream together the butter and sugar and mix in the beaten egg yolks, mashed sweet potatoes, sherry and seasonings. Fold in the egg whites and pour the mixture into a small buttered casserole dish. Bake at 350° for 30 to 40 minutes.

Makes 4 servings.

3	tablespoons butter
½	cup plus 2 tablespoons brown sugar
2	egg yolks, well beaten
3	medium sweet potatoes, peeled, boiled and mashed
¼	cup sherry
	Salt to taste
½	teaspoon freshly grated nutmeg
⅛	teaspoon mace
2	egg whites, stiffly beaten

the Dancing Master, leading us in minuets and reels, delicate dances where nuance is everything—from downcast eyes to pertly tilted chin. It's easy to forget how important a subtle flirtation used to be. These dances are formal, and more strenuous mentally—at least to the novice—than they are physically. After our feast, this is a boon.

Upton and I slip out during the Sir Roger deCoverly, the last dance of the evening. The snow is still lightly falling, and I wait outside the lighted windows of the gathering room while Upton brings the car around. I can hear the gentle tinkling music of the virginal, and it sounds far away, like fairy music. I stand on tiptoe and peer in the small-paned windows. What a vision it is, these gracious candlelit figures honoring each other with bows and curtseys, skirts swirling, gentlemen pointing their toes.

As I watch this, my final glimpse of the eighteenth century, I wonder whether, 200 years ago, others like ourselves might have celebrated similarly after all. The thought is so appealing—secret merrymakers dancing these same dances in these same old rooms, tucked away among the silent hills—that I decide to believe that eighteenth-century New Englanders did celebrate Christmas in this fashion. After all, who would have known?

CHAPTER EIGHT

COUNTRY CRAFTS
AND
HOLIDAY HANDIWORK

projects for the season

Meandering throughout New England, I am struck again and again by the multitude and diversity of craftspeople here— some of them full-time artisans who make their livings by their crafts, and others who create in their free time, for fun. People joke and say that the weather here is so horrible for so much of the time that there's nothing else to do but knit or cross-stitch or quilt, but I think it goes deeper than the weather.

We Yankees have a long history of industry and inventiveness. And we're also known to cling to our roots and traditions. If our grandmothers sewed quilts and knit socks beside the wood stove while the wind whistled and the snow collected on the window panes, well, why not us, too?

The women who have contributed to this chapter are not only skilled in executing their crafts but also are designers, and all the patterns here are original. The only drawback to working with these clever and energetic artists is that they are always moving on to other, newer projects. So I have had to learn to scoop up appealing handiwork the minute I find it and to get in touch with the maker as soon as I can, before the creator is off working on another idea.

All the crafts in this chapter call for some very basic knowledge of needlework—sewing, knitting, quilting or working a cross-stitch. The gnome (page 127) is the easiest. However, if you haven't done much sewing, the cross-stitch place mat (page 130) is a good place to begin. But all these projects require more time to complete than the ones found elsewhere in this book. Plan on spending, oh, at least a three-day blizzard or a week of long winter evenings by the fire.

MOUNTAIN LAKE SWEATER

Maine designer Lisa Wallace dreamed up and made the Mountain Lake Sweater for North Island Designs in North Haven, Maine, which was founded a few years ago by Chellie Pingree. Originally, several families on this small northern island raised sheep. Although the sheep have been moved to another island, they still provide the wool for the sweaters. Chellie and the seven other women who make up North Island Designs are all island dwellers who see knitting as "a chance to create your own island—yourself and the project, a feeling of total absorption, with an end product."

General Notes

• The pattern is for a 36-inch chest measurement, with directions for 40- and 44-inch sizes indicated in parentheses. For needles, use numbers 5 and 7, or whatever sizes are needed to get a stitch gauge of 4½ stitches = 1 inch using size 7 needles and knitting worsted wool. As usual, K stands for knit and P for purl.

• Read the charts from right to left on knit rows and from left to right on purl rows.

• Decreases: Make neck edge and sleeve decreases 2 stitches in from the edge to create a neat seam line. Use a K2tog (knit 2 together) decrease on the left edge of the neck and the end of the sleeve. Use a SSK (slip next 2 stitches as if to knit, put left needle into the front of the slipped stitches and knit them together) decrease on the right side of the neck and the beginning of the sleeve.

Materials

5 (6, 6) 4-ounce skeins burgundy yarn (main color)

1 4-ounce skein dark jade yarn (mountains)

1 4-ounce skein blue yarn (lake)

1 4-ounce skein light blue yarn (trees)

2 porcelain loon buttons (optional)

Knitting needles, sizes 5 and 7

Circular needle, size 5

1. *To make the front:* Using size 5 needles and the burgundy yarn, cast on 84 (92, 100) stitches. Work 1 row twisted rib (knit into the back of each knit stitch) for the bottom of the sweater. Then switch to the light blue yarn, and continuing in the twisted rib stitch, work for 2 inches.

2. Change to size 7 needles. Working a stockinette pattern (knit 1 row, purl 1 row; knit side is right side of sweater), follow the design chart for the front. When the front measures 13 (14, 15) inches, work 5 (5, 6) stitches at the beginning of the next row and place them on a holder. Work the remainder of the row until the last 5 (5, 6) stitches, and place them on a holder. These stitches mark the underarm.

3. Continue in stockinette stitch on 74 (82, 88) stitches for 6 (6¼, 6½) inches. End with a purl row. Begin the neck shaping (see below): Work across 26 (30, 33) stitches. Place the center 22 stitches on a holder. Attach a second ball of yarn and finish the row. Working both sides at the same time, decrease 1 stitch at the neck edge, every other row, 6 times, to get 20 (24, 27) shoulder stitches. At 8¾ (9, 9¼) inches above the underarm, slip the stitches to holders. These will be knit together with the back shoulder stitches.

4. *To make the back:* Follow the instructions for the front, but do not work the neck shaping. At 8¾ (9, 9¼) inches above the underarm, slip the stitches to three holders in groups as follows: size 36: 20, 34, 20; size 40: 24, 34, 24; size 44: 27, 34, 27.

5. *To make the shoulder seams and neck:* Knit the shoulder seams together by holding the front and back shoulder sections right sides together. Using a third needle, knit together the first stitch from each

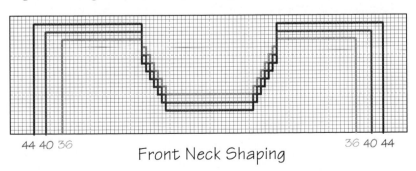

44 40 36   36 40 44
Front Neck Shaping

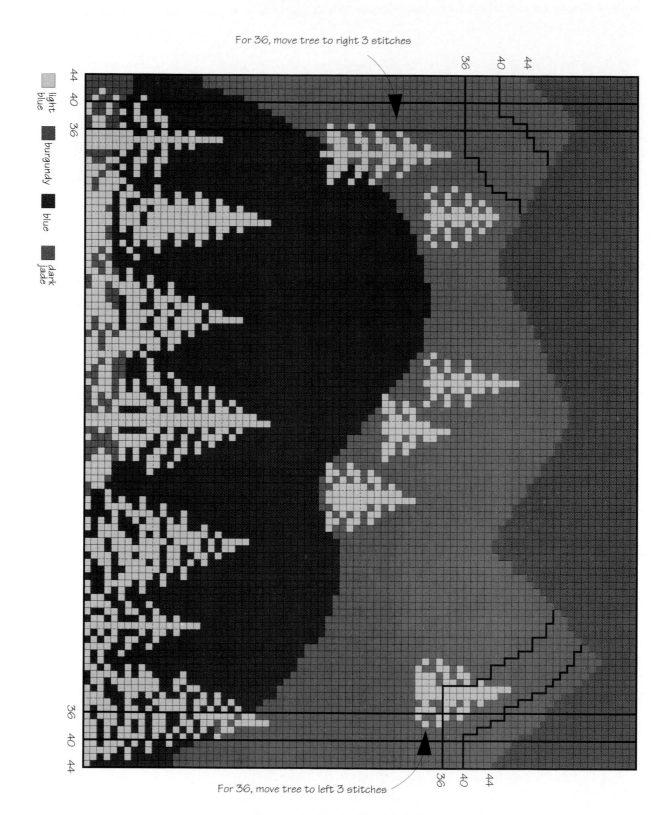

For 36, move tree to right 3 stitches

For 36, move tree to left 3 stitches

light
blue

burgundy

blue

dark
jade

Front "MOUNTAIN LAKE"

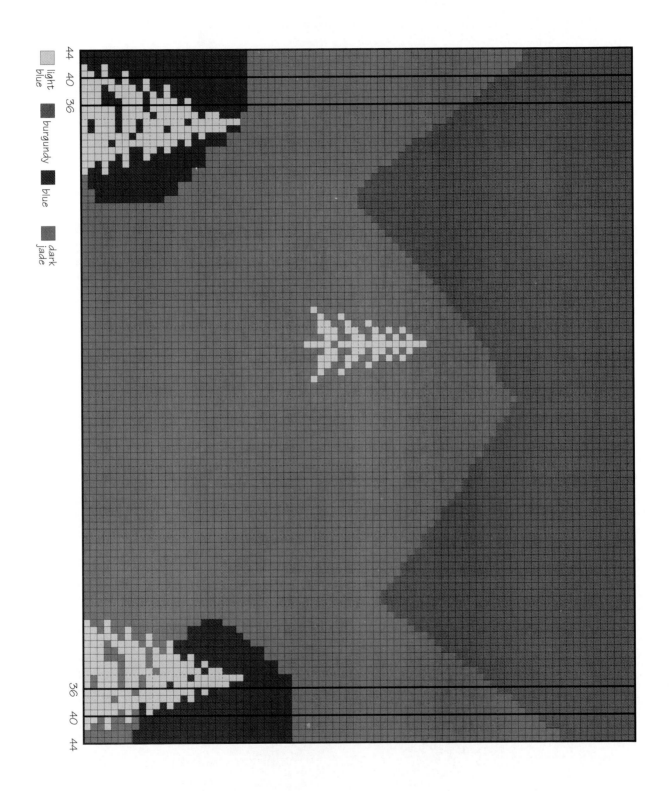

Back "MOUNTAIN LAKE"

needle. Knit together the second stitches and bind off the first. Continue to knit together and bind off all the shoulder stitches.

6. Using a size 5 circular needle and the jade yarn, beginning at the right shoulder with the right side facing, knit across 34 stitches on the back neck holder, pick up 15 stitches down the left neck edge, knit 22 stitches from the front neck holder and pick up 15 stitches up the right front neck edge. You will have 86 stitches on your needle. Work 3 rows in twisted rib, then bind off all stitches. Use a larger needle for binding off if you tend to bind off too tightly.

7. *To make the sleeves:* Using size 7 needles and the burgundy yarn, and with the right side facing you, knit 5 (5, 6) stitches from the underarm holder, pick up evenly 76 (78, 80) stitches from body to the other holder. Knit stitches from the holder, making a total of 86 (88, 92) stitches. Work in stockinette pattern for 3 rows. Decrease 1 stitch at each edge of the needle on the next row and then every sixth row. Work for 16 (16½, 17) inches, ending with a knit row. Decrease evenly across the next row to 36 (36, 40) stitches. Switch to a size 5 needle and work in twisted rib until the sleeve length measures 17¾ (18¼, 18¾) inches. Switch to the jade yarn, work 1 row and bind off all stitches.

8. *To finish:* Block each section. Sew the side and sleeve seams with right sides together, using a backstitch. Weave in all ends. If you like, sew loon buttons on the lake.

SAINT NICHOLAS DOLL

Faith Kolodziejski is a Cape Cod artist who has created such a throng of whimsical creatures from natural materials that she is now writing a book about them. One of my favorites is this 20-inch-high Saint Nicholas in mufti, relaxing after a busy season. There's a bit of the woodland about him—note the pinecones on his hood—but take a close look at the photograph on page 126, and you'll see he really is a Santa Claus after all.

1. *To make the body:* Enlarge the body pattern to full size following the instructions in "How to Enlarge a Pattern" on page 14. Trace two patterns onto the muslin. Cut out the front and back, adding ¼-inch seam allowances as you cut. Sew the front and back together, leaving the bottom open. Trim the seams and turn right side out. Stuff the body firmly with fiberfill, stopping about three-quarters of the way down. Fill the sandwich bag with sand or cat litter, then knot the bag. Stuff this into the body, then fill it the rest of the way with fiberfill. Cut a round of cardboard the same size as the base of the body. Cut a piece of muslin 1 inch larger than the cardboard. Glue the muslin to the cardboard, wrapping the edges over and gluing them securely. Slipstitch this base to the bottom of the body.

2. *To paint the features:* Mix your paints with fabric medium (4 parts paint to 1 part medium). Paint the hands and face tan, giving them

Materials
½ yard muslin
½ yard tweed fabric
1 yard burgundy wool fabric (36" × 44")
Polyester fiberfill
Sand or cat litter
Sandwich bag
Heavy cardboard
Household glue
Tan, white, blue, brown and black acrylic paint
Fabric medium (available at craft stores)
Varnish
Fine-tipped paintbrush
Wide-tipped paintbrush
Remnant of fur (4" × 52")
Scraps of trim or braid

two coats if necessary. When painting, let each color dry completely before adding the next. Lightly sketch the facial features with a pencil. Then paint the whites of the eyes; when these dry, paint the center of the eyes blue. Paint a brown nose and eyelashes. Paint the pupils with a dab of black paint. Dip a paintbrush into the pink paint, wipe off most of the paint on a cloth and add a trace of color to the cheeks. When all the paint is completely dry, add a coat of varnish to the whole body.

3. *To make the coat:* Enlarge the coat pattern to full size as you did for the body. Trace two coat patterns onto the tweed. Cut out the front and back, adding ¼-inch seam allowances as you cut. Sew the front and back together with right sides facing, leaving the bottom, top and sleeves open. Turn right side out. Turn the neck edges under ¼ inch, and using a double thread, run a gathering stitch around the neck opening, beginning and ending at the center back point of the neck. Leave long ends on this thread. Repeat the process for each sleeve.

4. *To fit the coat:* Dress Saint Nicholas in his coat. Pull the gathering threads on the neck and sleeves until they fit tightly. Tie off the gathering threads and trim the ends.

5. *To trim the coat:* If the fur you use tends to unravel, you may want to hem the edges. Cut the 52-inch fur remnant into two pieces, 34 inches and 18 inches. Tack the short piece of fur to the center front of the coat and the long piece to the bottom of the coat as shown in the photograph on page 126. Sew the decorative trim to the cuffs.

6. *To add the hair:* For each eyebrow, roll a tiny bit of the wool roving between your finger and thumb until the brow is the size you want. Using a long needle, sew the brows on, bringing the needle out through the back of the head and then back through to the front (these stitches will be covered by his hair later). For the beard, make sure you have enough wool roving for a full, fluffy beard, and lay it across Saint Nick's face from his forehead to his chin. Secure the beard with a few stitches just below his nose, using the sewing technique you used for the brows. Then flip the beard down and tack it into place with a few loose stitches (tight stitches will make the beard less full and fluffy).

For the hair, start with some short, curly pieces of wool for bangs, and tack these into place around the face. Then, starting at the crown of the head, take a small piece of the wool roving, fold it in half and tack it to the head at the fold. Repeat this, working from the top of the head down and from front to back, until Saint Nicholas has a very full head of hair.

7. *To finish the doll:* Drape the burgundy fabric over Saint Nicholas's head for his cape, tying a piece of raffia around his neck to secure the hood. Glue the small pinecones, bits of greenery and twigs to the hood. Glue a small pinecone, a bit of dried orange peel, some raffia and a chestnut to the large cinnamon stick. Add a bow made from the green ribbon, then glue the cinnamon stick staff to Saint Nicholas's hand. Our Saint Nick is carrying a bag made of pillow ticking filled with nuts and twigs; add a sack to your Saint Nick, too, if you like.

Large handful curly wool roving

Handful of raffia

Glue gun

4 or 5 small pinecones

Pinch of greenery and twigs

Few pieces of dried orange peel

Chestnut

Large (12") cinnamon stick

12" of green ribbon

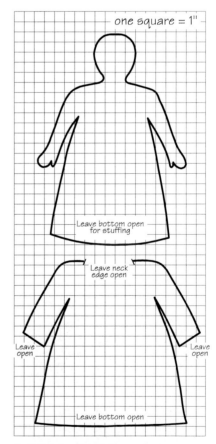

Body (top) and coat (bottom) patterns for Saint Nicholas Doll.

CHRISTMAS GNOME

Cape Cod native Faith Kolodziejski brushed the fluffy moustaches and sent me a pair of these gnomes for company during the Christmas season. I'm not absolutely positive, but it seems that since the gnomes arrived, things like cookies and Christmas candies vanish overnight, and my measuring spoons and sewing scissors keep turning up in the oddest places. Faith says she is indebted to Kahlin, a seven-year-old sprite who first saw the gnomes and introduced Faith to them and to the world of magic.

1. *To make the body:* Enlarge the gnome pattern using the instructions in "How to Enlarge a Pattern" on page 14 and trace one onto each piece of muslin. Cut out the gnome front and back, adding ¼-inch seam allowances as you cut. Sew the front and back together, leaving the bottom open. Trim the seams and turn the gnome right side out.

2. Stuff the gnome firmly with fiberfill, stopping about three-quarters of the way down. Place sand or cat litter into the sandwich bag, then knot the bag. Stuff this into the bottom of the gnome, then fill him the rest of the way with additional fiberfill. Cut a round of cardboard the same size as the base of the gnome. Cut a piece of muslin ¼ inch larger than the cardboard. Glue the muslin to the cardboard, wrapping the edges over and gluing them securely. Slipstitch this base to the bottom of the gnome.

3. *To paint the gnome:* Lightly sketch the gnome's features with a pencil. When painting, let each color dry completely before adding the next. Paint the hat red. Paint the face tan, giving it two coats if necessary. Paint the body blue. Paint the bottom blue as well. Using a fine brush, paint the nose brown. Then paint the whites of the eyes; when these dry, paint the center of the eyes blue or brown. Dip a paintbrush into the pink paint, wipe off most of the paint on a cloth and add a trace of color to the cheeks. When all the paint is completely dry, add a coat of varnish to the entire gnome.

4. *To add the hair:* For each eyebrow, roll a tiny bit of the lambs' wool between your finger and thumb until the brow is about ½ inch long. Form clumps of wool into a beard and hair. To attach the hair, beard, and eyebrows, thread a needle with thread that matches the color of the wool. Sew the hair on with tiny stitches that pass through to the back of the gnome's head. Attach the hair so that it covers the stitches in the back.

Saint Nicholas, with his faithful Gnomes in attendance.

Materials

2 pieces of muslin (4" × 10" or larger)

Polyester fiberfill

Sand or cat litter

Sandwich bag

Cardboard

Scrap of muslin (2" × 2")

Household glue

Red, tan, blue, brown, white and pink fabric paint

Varnish

Fine-tipped paintbrush

Wide-tipped paintbrush

Lambs' wool

Pattern for Christmas Gnome.

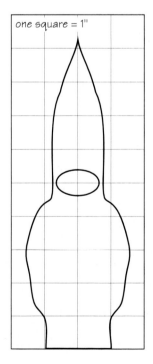

one square = 1"

QUILTED TREE SKIRT

My friend Bobbie Ward cannot keep her needle still and goes from one quilting project to another. Fortunately, she loves to teach. Near her home in Bedford, Massachusetts, many talented sewers have been enriched by her patient help. Bobbie's tree skirt has an appealing array of teddy bears to watch over gift-opening on Christmas morning—perfect for a child's tabletop tree! The finished skirt is approximately 25 inches in diameter.

1. Enlarge the pattern on the opposite page and transfer it to heavy paper or cardboard using the instructions in "How to Enlarge a Pattern" on page 14. Cut apart the pattern to make separate pattern pieces B through G.

2. Trace eight of each piece (except the A panel) onto your various print fabrics, arranging the different prints to suit your taste. Make sure to add ¼-inch seam allowances to all sides of each piece when you cut them out.

3. *To piece the blocks:* Sew pieces B and C to either side of the center panel A. Add pieces D and E, as shown in the block diagram on the opposite page. Then add pieces F and G to the sides. Make eight blocks. Press all the seams toward the darker fabric as you go.

Materials

¾ **yard total of assorted holiday prints for blocks and binding**

8 center panels, 3½" × 4¼" (pattern piece A; ours in the photo are teddy bears)

¾ **yard red print material for backing**

¾ **yard flat, lightweight batting**

1 yard red ribbon (optional)

Delightful teddy bears dance under a table-top Christmas tree on this festive skirt.

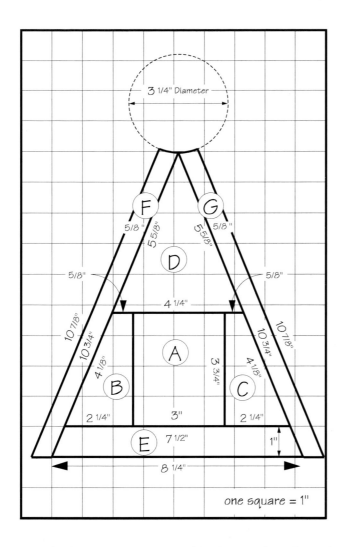

Patterns and block diagram for Quilted Tree Skirt.

4. *To assemble the skirt top:* Sew the blocks together along the long sides, making an octagon. Leave one seam unsewn, as shown at right.

5. Using the pieced top as a pattern, cut the backing and batting pieces to match. Make a cut from the edge to the center on both the backing and the batting along the unsewn seam in the pieced top. Cut a 3¼-inch hole in the center of the batting and backing.

6. *To assemble the tree skirt:* Layer the backing and skirt top with right sides together, then add the batting on top. If you want to add ribbon ties, insert two 18-inch lengths of ribbon between the backing and pieced layer just below the center hole. The raw edges should be even, and keep the ribbon to the inside, out of the way of the stitching lines. Making sure the cuts in all three pieces line up precisely, pin the layers together and baste. Sew a continuous seam, starting and stopping where indicated in the illustration at right, leaving an opening to turn the skirt right side out.

7. Turn the skirt, slipstitch the opening closed and quilt as desired.

Note: All seams are ¼ inch.

Layer the backing, skirt top and batting. Sew around the edges, leaving one edge open for turning.

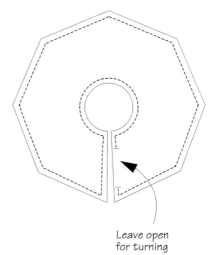

Leave open for turning

HOLIDAY PLACE MAT

Before her daughter was born, Amy Harrison Casey had never counted a single cross-stitch. But by the time her daughter was one year old, Amy had begun to create her own designs. Her first cross-stitch patterns were of favorite historic New England houses—no small feat for someone who had never drawn or painted before. Now she has moved on to more whimsical designs such as those on the "Merry Christmas" place mat shown on the opposite page.

General Notes

• Each cross-stitch is made up of two slanting stitches (Figure 1). Each cross is worked in holes woven into the fabric. Cross-stitch is not done one square at a time. Work left to right stitching half of an X, then right to left to complete the stitch. To make the stitches as shown, come up at A and down at B; then up at C and down at D; then up at E and down at B; then up at C and down at F.

• Backstitching is used to outline and is indicated on the design charts (page 132) by straight, heavy lines. Use one strand of dark brown for outlining everything except the letters. Use one strand of red to outline the letters. Use two strands of black for the runners and handles of the sleighs. Some of the lines on the chart are long; be sure to break your stitches so that they are not longer than five squares. To make the outline stitches as shown (Figure 2), come up at A and down at B; then up at C and down at A; then up at D and down at C.

Cross-Stitch Directions

1. Use three strands for all cross-stitch work.

2. Cut the floss into 18-inch pieces before using. Never knot the floss; leave a ½-inch tail and secure it by working the first few stitches over it. Slip the end of your floss (about ½ inch) under existing stitches when you finish with a color.

3. Begin by locating your first stitch (the top left stitch in the H). Place this stitch in the middle column of your fabric. (To find the middle, fold the long side of your fabric in half.) Allow a minimum of 2 inches or 28 squares for your edges, then place your first stitch. Continue counting from the chart to complete your design.

4. Hand wash the fabric with a mild detergent such as Ivory or Woolite. It is important to wash your design after it is completed so that the holes in the fabric will close. Mix a small amount of detergent in warm water and gently agitate the fabric for a few minutes. Rinse gently in warm water. Remove the fabric, but *do not wring!* Lay the fabric flat on a dishtowel. Place another dishtowel over the fabric to remove excess water. When the fabric is only slightly damp, press it with an iron on the medium-low (no steam) setting, placing a thin piece of fabric, such as a handkerchief, over your fabric. Press very carefully.

5. Once your design is washed, trim the margin down to 10 squares away from the design. Cut your batting and backing fabric to match.

Materials

14-count antique white Aida cross-stitch fabric (14" × 19½")

Tapestry needle

Embroidery floss, 1 skein each white, black, dark brown, silver, red, medium green, dark green, blue, brown and yellow

Lightweight batting (14" × 19½")

Backing fabric (14" × 19½")

2 yards dark green ½" double-fold bias tape

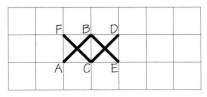

Figure 1. Basic cross-stitch technique.

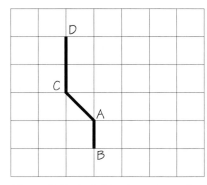

Figure 2. Backstitching is used to outline.

Cross-stitched bells, holly and snowmen border this Holiday Place Mat.

Stitch the bias tape around the edge of your design, right sides together, folding the corners under neatly. Place the design face down, place the batting and backing on top, pin the bias tape securely to the edges and hand stitch the place mat together.

Note: Whenever you need to wash your completed place mat, be sure to wash by hand using warm water and a mild detergent.

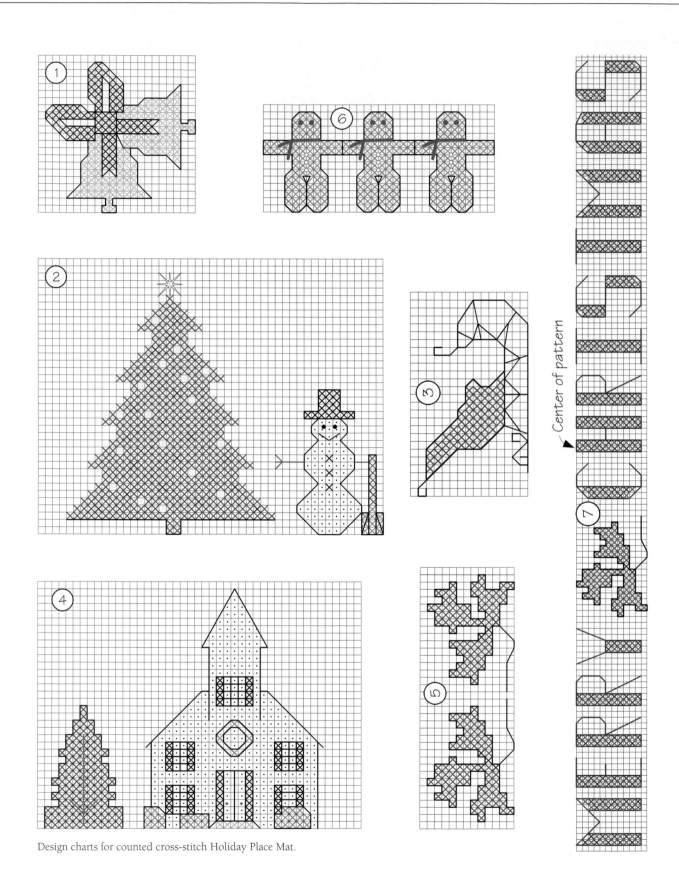

Design charts for counted cross-stitch Holiday Place Mat.

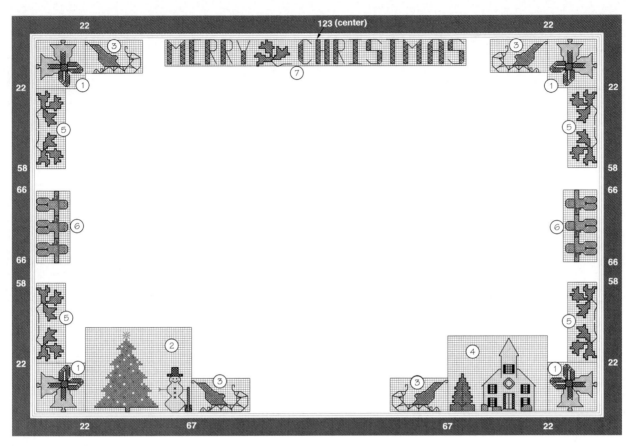

Pattern for Holiday Place Mat.

Chart Notes

• The squares on the charts correspond to the fabric squares. Each square represents one cross-stitch, and each color represents the floss from the color key at right.

• Green Mix is one strand of medium green and two strands of dark green.

• \ Indicates ½ of a cross-stitch.

• Straight heavy lines indicate backstitching.

	Color	DMC number
·	White	
■	Black	310
■	Dark brown	3371
▢	Silver	648
■	Red	304
▨	Medium green	701
■	Dark Green	986
■	Blue	930
▨	Brown	433
▨	Green mix	(see Notes)
▢	Yellow	676

CHAPTER NINE

A CHRISTMAS STORY

the bells of christmas

❦

"*J*ust forget it, okay?" Max's voice was tight as a wire, and he would not look at me. He just stared at the table, small shoulders stiff with anger, fingers tearing off bits of Christmas napkin from the third-grade party where they'd told him the truth.

I shrugged. "Okay, I'll forget it," I said, thinking, but what about you, Max? I looked at his little sister, Lily, not quite five and very full of Santa Claus this year. When Max started ranting, Lily had rather deliberately climbed down from her chair and was now off in the pantry crouched beside the box of kittens, stroking them and crooning softly. Did she know what he was talking about?

Max and Lily's parents had separated last spring. The children and Sophie, their mother, had stayed on in the farmhouse across the field from our house, and when Sophie was lucky enough to land a job teaching art at a suburban high school 20 miles away, I'd volunteered to keep Max and Lily after school every day until she got home. I kind of liked having small children around again. It kept me from feeling guilty about not having gotten a real job now that my own five were so grown up. Max and Lily had chores just like everyone else. Max mucked out the ponies' stalls and fed them, with the help of Nell—my baby, now 12—and Lily did the chickens with Eliza—my oldest, now a senior in high school. Of course, Max's real heroes were the three big boys, 15-year-old Andrew in particular. They'd roughhouse with him, teach him all sorts of good and, I'm sure, not-so-good things. Mainly they kept Max in line.

And Max was one tough customer. Angry. Even mean. At least that's what I'd begun to think lately. I gave him another couple of cookies and refilled his glass with milk and still he didn't look at me or stop shredding his napkin. His tense, bony little back looked so frail under his plaid shirt, his neck so smooth and vulnerable where his hair swirled down in two silky points above his collar, that I couldn't resist putting my hands on either side of his neck, just for a minute, the way you gentle a horse. Only I didn't feel him soften even slightly beneath my touch, and suddenly I wished the school bus would hurry up with the big boys before Max's thunderstorm broke. They would know just how to deal with this shattered faith. And of course, they did, the minute they got in.

"What's this, no Santa Claus?"

"You think it's your mother?"

"So prove it, Max."

"Yeah, prove it."

Poor Max, looking up to find five pairs of eyes challenging him from across the kitchen table. "Well, okay. Okay, I will." His face became flushed. Nell jumped up quickly and took Lily and the kittens into the living room, softly closing the door behind her. The rest of us waited for Max to let go.

"On Christmas Eve, after we hang up our stockings and lock the doors, after we go upstairs, I'll make a giant spider's web with lots of string, all across the hall to the stairs. I'll fix it so there's no way she can get back downstairs without wrecking it." He looked at us triumphantly. "And then...and then I'll bring my sleeping bag, and Lily's, too, into Mom's bedroom. We'll sleep right next to her bed, and I'll lock that door, too, and keep the key. That's it, that's what I'll do."

At first nobody, not even Andrew, said anything.

It was a horrible plot, and Sophie would be feeling just guilty enough about the kids to go along with it. I started to say something, to protest and try to reason with Max, but Andrew put up a silencing hand. Amazing how big it was all of a sudden, a man's hand on a still-slender boy's wrist.

"I think that's a great scheme there, Max." Andrew's voice seemed deeper, too. "If the stockings are still empty Christmas morning, no Santa, right?"

Max nodded.

"Of course, no presents either."

"I mean no stocking presents. I already know my Dad's giving me skis. My Dad. Not Santa."

"So all we have to do is talk your mother into this, right?"

Max nodded again.

"Andrew," I began again, but he gave me another stern look, and somehow I knew then he had his own plan cooking.

After Max and Lily left, he explained. "It's easy, Mom. Two stockings to a pair, right? One to hang up, empty, and one for Sophie to stuff early and bring here, full. On Christmas Eve, we just sneak in and switch them. Nothing to it." His face shone with success, the way it had when he first learned to ride his bike so long ago, and my heart jumped a little. I had to admit, it was a great idea, and when he told Sophie, she was entranced.

Max and Lily conveniently spent the weekend with Will, their father, giving harried, hurried Sophie a breather, and a chance to stuff the stockings in private. She brought them over Sunday afternoon; Monday was Christmas Eve. The stockings were big. And they were bulging. An old-fashioned china doll peeked shyly out of the top of Lily's, and Max's swelled with an old, well-polished hunting horn of real brass. Kabuki-like masks, painted by Sophie, hovered on sticks above each stocking, with long shiny streamers drifting down. They were stockings that held real treasures; anyone could tell that.

"I love to do the Santa part of Christmas," confided Sophie, arranging the streamers. "Will goes for the big, showy stuff, dolls with factory-made acrylic wardrobes and complete ski packages. That's okay, I guess. But I like to give people things they never even dreamed of."

She fingered a tiny tea set with roses so small I had to squint to see them. "This cost $1.50, and then I painted on the roses." Sophie slid the teapot and four snowflake-sized cups and saucers into a flowery pouch about as big as my finger and tucked it behind the doll. Lucky little Lily, lucky Max.

She passed her hand over each stocking, almost like a kind of benediction, and turned to Andrew. "So that's it. Here's a basket of candy and a few more presents to tie on the tree if you don't get caught. And the key will be on the angel." Andrew nodded. For Christmas last year she'd made two terra-cotta angels, one for us, and we both had them mounted beside our front doors and hid our keys between the wings. "Well, then, good luck, Andrew." Sophie stood on tiptoe and stretched to kiss his cheek. "And thanks. I always knew you were my man." I watched as first the smile and then a pink flush washed across his face.

"Yeah, well, keep your fingers crossed and Max in bed."

Christmas Eve was clear and cold and white, the big church packed with candles and dozing babies. This year, with both sets of grandparents along, our household filled an entire pew. We sang Glo-o-o-o-oria, pitting our impoverished voices against those of the silver-throated choristers, and once warmed up, we warbled most of the way home.

After midnight on Christmas Eve, a potent magic falls. The houses are dark except for twinkling Christmas lights, and the world feels solid with sleep, as if we are the only ones awake. Andrew and I, both a little apprehensive, peered at Sophie's house as we drove past. It, too, looked sleep-drenched and peaceful. Ready for Santa.

It was just after one o'clock when we left our house for Sophie's, going through the barn to give the ponies sugar lumps and a Christmas bonus of oats, and the barn cats a bowl of warm milk. I wondered as I always do on Christmas Eve if the animals had talked in the witching hour between midnight and one. The ponies snuffled up the sugar, velvet noses grazing my palms, and I thought they did look as though they shared a secret.

At the threshold of the barn, Andrew set the basket down, handed me the stockings and without a word, vanished into the tack room, emerging seconds later with Bucky's harness bells around his neck. Eight jumbo jingle bells and two swinging clapper bells, all brass and each with a different jangle, were stitched to a thick sheepskin yoke trimmed with red leather. Andrew gave the bells a quick shake, and the ponies stopped their thoughtful munching, ears pricked up, alert to this cheerful sound.

"C'mon, Mom. We're off. I'll switch the stockings, and while I

do that, you tie the stuff on the tree." He took the stockings and trotted off, the bells chink-chinking softly to his tread, the merest hint of reindeer.

I have never stolen into a slumbering house other than my own on Christmas Eve. It is wonderful, breathtaking and unlike anything else. My heart skipped fast as Andrew quietly laid down the bells on a snowbank, groped for the key and stealthily slid it into the keyhole. The door swung open into a dusty, twinkling warmth. I could just make out the threads of Max's clumsy web tangled tightly across the stairs.

We worked fast as lightning, stopping only once or twice when we heard the old house creak. I felt as though I were part of another people, invisible and charmed. When we were finished, we stepped back and looked, spellbound by what we had done. There was a rustle upstairs, a sleepy sigh. Andrew and I both started toward the door and then Andrew stopped short, reaching out a long arm toward the hearth. Milk and cookies and a note. "OH SANTA I try to be good LOVE LILY." The letters were shaky and

slanted and careful. Andrew polished off the milk and cookies while I absently put the note back on the table. But Andrew with a fierce look snatched it up again, borrowed a candy-cane pen sticking out of Max's stocking and scrawled on the back: "Good cookies, thanks, Merry Christmas!" Oh, he really had the knack of it, this Christmas magic.

Outside, he relocked the door, picked up the bells and took off, circling the house twice in the shadow of the pine trees and letting the bells really go in a joyful jangle. Then together we dashed toward home, the bells just spilling out in the moonlight, over the cold, white fields.

On Christmas afternoon, Sophie came over after Will had picked up the children. She said that Max had been jubilant when he'd seen the bulging stockings, the candy and new presents tied on the tree, the empty milk glass, the note. He found out he was wrong, and it was as if a great sorrow had been lifted.

Suddenly, he had permission to believe in whatever he wanted to, said Sophie. She paused for a minute and took a quick breath. Then she looked at me, eyes wide. "And something else wonderful happened last night." She went to the window. "I heard sleigh bells, a little after midnight. I know I did."

"I heard them too, Sophie," I said. And we stood there at the window, shoulder to shoulder, each of us remembering how our hearts had quickened, our spirits lifted with the glad chink-chink of bells across the silvery fields.

PHOTO CREDITS

INDEX

NOTE: Page references in **boldface** indicate photographs. *Italic* references indicate illustrations.